Dirt Ordinary
Shining a Light on Conspiracies

Shining a Light Series

Dirt Ordinary: Shining a Light on Conspiracies, by Rod Martin, Jr.
Favorable Incompetence: Shining a Light on 9/11, by Rod Martin, Jr.
Thermophobia: Shining a Light on Global Warming, by Rod Martin, Jr.

Climate Basics series

Climate Basics: Nothing to Fear, by Rod Martin, Jr.—an Amazon #1 Bestseller in Weather and Science & Math Short Reads.
Deserts & Droughts: How Does Land Ever Get Water? by Rod Martin, Jr.

Dirt Ordinary
Shining a Light on Conspiracies

Rod Martin, Jr.

Shining a Light *series*

Tharsis Highlands Publishing
Cebu, Philippines

Published by Tharsis Highlands Publishing
Cebu, Philippines
https://tharsishighlands.wordpress.com/books/

Amazon Print Edition
June 2019
ISBN: 9781075907173

EBook Editions
Amazon Kindle—2016, 2018
Smashwords—2015, 2018

Front cover photo: H.R. Haldeman and John Ehrlichman, of Watergate infamy, discuss policy on board Air Force One, 1973 (PD) via Wikimedia.org. Three days later, they are asked to resign by President Nixon.
Back cover: Hands shaking with Euro bank notes, photo by Kiwiev (CC0). Students on their ways to class, photo by University of the Fraser Valley (CC BY 2.0). Airplane hits World Trade Center, South Tower on September 11, 2001, photo by Robert J. Fisch (CC BY-SA 2.0). Sex worker posing for the camera, photo by Cascari Juhu (CC BY-SA 3.0).
Cover design: Rod Martin, Jr.

Typography fonts
Headings: Rockwell Extra Bold
Running Heads: Rockwell
Text: Palatino Linotype

"Power tends to corrupt, and absolute power corrupts absolutely. Great men are almost always bad men." —Lord Acton (Letter to Mandell Creighton, April 5, 1887)

Table of Contents

Introduction:
Conspiracies are Dirt Ordinary

Bright green flooded the space between buildings, and the December sun poured down upon metropolitan Cebu. Inside the solitary structure of a modern, four-year college, classes of students ignored the heat beyond their air-conditioned rooms.

One of those students asked a provocative question of his American professor—your author—about politics in the United States. I admitted that there had been some evidence of corruption in America. I gave Watergate as an example.

"Was that a conspiracy?" asked the student.

For a moment, something shifted in my mind. I felt a knot in my stomach, a subtle tightness across my body, combined with a brief urge to flee. I felt the awkwardness of exposure, without knowing its source.

The next moment, I became critically aware of those feelings. A sense of anxiety faded as I looked inward at my own thoughts.

I had become aware of an automatic response to the word "conspiracy"—a knee-jerk reaction that took me entirely by surprise.

"Yes," I replied. "That incident was a perfect example of a conspiracy and the crime which followed."

Over the next few months, I had the good fortune to explore this topic even further. In my professional ethics class for college seniors, I observed that none of my students had my reaction to the word or topic. Was this merely a personal weakness on my part—a flaw in my own character?

Was my reaction an anomaly? Or was it purely an American phenomenon?

In my class preparation, I came across the videos of a researcher who had experienced something similar. He had found that the citizens of Europe and some Third World countries were equally relaxed with the conspiracy concept, while Americans suffered an automatic block on the subject.

Many Americans claimed to be skeptics, while ridiculing anyone who talked of such things, but those supposed skeptics showed none of the restraint and humility of a true scientist. In America, ridicule of conspiracy talk had become habitual (Storm Clouds Gathering).

I poured over dozens of hours of YouTube videos. More than once, I saw newscasters and show hosts roll their eyes at the mention of some controversial topic.

One acerbic host wouldn't wait for his guest to finish speaking. He would lambaste his guest with something like, *You nut! You're a loony toon—tin-foil conspiracy crackpot.*

Throughout the worst of them, what distressed me most was the non-sequitur nature of the hosts' responses. A guest might mention a controversial fact or raise a provocative question, but all too frequently, these were referred to as "conspiracy theories."

Were the hosts so unintelligent that they didn't know the difference between theory and fact, or conspiracy and question? Had show hosts become so blind and belligerent that they could not ask for clarification? Was this some group delusion that had come to grip the American news media? Or was there some natural or artificial force molding their attitudes and speech?

It might prove helpful to find answers to these questions, but we won't be answering them in this book. We will, however, look at the common nature of conspiracies. We will show that ridicule is not warranted, at least most of the time. Some conspiracy theories are based on facts, instead of imagination or delusion. These days, however, the corporate media has made it fashionable to ridicule facts, questions and even the search for truth.

It should be noted that a suspicious nature is only paranoia if it is unreasonable—based upon delusion or imagination. If suspicions are based upon facts, that is an entirely different animal. More and more, all suspicions are called "paranoia" in error. Both movies and corporate media are feeding this inaccurate view of things. And the public who view these movies and media repeat that behavior so that it becomes a self-reinforcing phenomenon. Another important question not to be covered in this book involves the reason why movies so consistently refer to all suspicion as paranoia. Is it by accident? A new social norm for the definition? Where did that norm crop up? Who originated it and why? Suspicion = paranoia = insanity. This false chain of equalities is inadvertently creating a kind of blindness.

The Cost of Conspiracies

In the twentieth century, documented conspiracies resulted in the deaths of 142.2 million people. This includes every major, and many minor wars throughout that hundred year period. But that's only for wars. Millions of other deaths have resulted from corporate conspiracies, gang and organized crime conspiracies and many other types of conspiracies.

But what really are conspiracies? Quite simply, they are conversations. A conspiracy happens when two or more people talk about doing something unethical or illegal. Like all evil, the perpetrators want their plans to remain shrouded in darkness, until at least the plan is so well along that nothing can stop it. Even then, the perpetrators frequently want to protect their own carcasses from prosecution.

For instance, Hitler might not have been successful in taking over the German government so thoroughly, if everyone suddenly knew that the Reichstag fire had been created by his own thugs, instead of a lone Communist patsy.

John F. Kennedy might have finished out his presidency and lived to a ripe old age, if E. Howard Hunt had gotten cold feet before the "Big Event" in Dallas, instead of waiting until his death bed to confess his small part in that crime. Perhaps the meme of "lone gunman" would never have gained traction in the minds of Americans.

If Woodward and Bernstein, of the *Washington Post*, had not become increasingly suspicious of the Watergate conspiracy, President Nixon might have finished out his second term, and Carter may not have become the next elected president.

Rockefeller Conspiracies

According to unverified sources, David Rockefeller is supposed to have thanked several news outlets for their discretion in keeping secret the plans of the New World Order. The following quote, supposedly made by Rockefeller, was purportedly given at a Bilderberg Group meeting, June 1991, in Baden-Baden, Germany.

"We are grateful to The Washington Post, The New York Times, Time magazine and other great publications whose directors have attended our meetings and respected their promises of discretion for almost forty years.... It would have been impossible for us to develop our plan for the world if we had been subject to the bright lights of publicity during those years. But, the world is now much more sophisticated and prepared to march towards a world government. The supranational sovereignty of an intellectual elite and world bankers is surely preferable to the national auto-determination practiced in past centuries."

"Bright lights of publicity?" Shining a light on evil is a good thing, so long as we don't become fixated on that evil or attempt to "resist" it. The light of awareness and Truth helps to shrivel up evil. But was Rockefeller's secret about something evil?

And did he really say these words? We may never know for certain. What David Rockefeller wrote twelve years later, in his *Memoirs*, sounds hauntingly similar in its meaning and intent.

"For more than a century, ideological extremists at either end of the political spectrum have seized upon well-publicized incidents such as my encounter with Castro to attack the Rockefeller family for the inordinate influence they claim we wield over American political and economic institutions. Some even believe we are part of a secret cabal working against the best interests of the United States, characterizing my family and me as 'internationalists' and of conspiring with others around the world to build a more integrated global political and economic structure—one world, if you will. If that is the charge, I stand guilty, and I am proud of it."

So, Rockefeller lists the charges and happily pleads guilty. Among those charges is a clear intent to commit treason in the dissolution of the United States. He also admits to conspiracy to commit this treason. But like so many of the rich and powerful, he will not go to jail for this admission. Too many minions in high places seem to agree with his intentions.

Orwellian Past, Unknown Future

In 1948, George Orwell wrote and published a book called *Nineteen Eighty-Four*, signifying the year. In that book, he told of a far different world where consolidation had greatly reduced the number of countries. The nation which included the former Great Britain—Oceania—was ruled by someone known by the euphemism, "Big Brother." The world of Oceania was one of perpetual war and never-ending government surveillance. Sound familiar? Today, we have a never-ending War on Terror and perpetual NSA surveillance.

One of the unique concepts introduced in that book was called Newspeak, a trimmed-down English with a greatly reduced vocabulary. This allowed for a form of thought control. How? If the words for concepts did not exist, then it became increasingly difficult to think them. Thus, such words as "rights," and "liberty" no longer existed. Effectively, the citizens became blind to those ideas.

Another artifact of this fictional culture was called "doublethink." Citizens were trained to accept two mutually contradictory beliefs without suffering any form of cognitive dissonance or emotional discomfort. For example, "war is peace." Others included, "ignorance is strength," and "freedom is slavery." Such concepts were reinforced by peer pressure and government brainwashing programs.

Orwell's book was published at the beginning of the Cold War, when the Soviet Union was increasingly characterized as totalitarian and evil.

Fast forward a few years, and the American press had started to call its wars, "peacekeeping actions." And over the next few decades, conspiracy theories would become thought of as crackpot or worthy of a "tinfoil hat."

As in Orwell's book, peer pressure within the American society has made the ridicule of truth, of true skepticism and of facts, a self-reinforcing phenomenon.

Distortions of Language

The word "discrimination" used to mean, "the act of distinguishing differences." It also used to mean, "the ability to make or perceive distinctions; perception; discernment." Each of these ideas refers to a positive trait of intelligence. These definitions still exist, but they have fallen largely into disuse. Now, the word "discrimination" has become an evil, negative idea meaning prejudice and bias, resulting in partiality and the unfair treatment of individuals. The thought of intelligence has become hidden behind prejudice. Was this accidental or by design?

These days, blame and responsibility have become synonymous, but there remains a big difference between these concepts. Blame is a negative attitude usually of shifting the burden from self to someone else so that they are made to suffer. Responsibility, on the other hand, is a positive attitude of taking control for the benefit of others. In a world where no one takes responsibility, and thinks only in terms of blame, a rare few can move in and take control more easily. Yet, selfish control is not responsibility, either.

Faith and belief have also become synonymous in many people's minds. There is an immense divergence between them. Belief is imperfect. Anyone can believe a lie and become fooled. Faith, on the other hand, is perfect and only relates to Absolute Truth. Regrettably, this is a rare state of being that few in the modern world have experienced. Thus, many believe it doesn't exist. Faith is the source of miracles—not the ordinary miracles of awe and mystery, or even accidental coincidence, but the extraordinary miracles of cause-and-effect coincidence, transcending the laws of physical reality. Shackled by mortal belief, few will ever see true faith. This is regrettable, because we could use a lot more faith in the world.

Love has become a battered term. In today's culture, it has turned out to be synonymous with lust and many other forms of selfishness. The true form of love is the opposite of selfishness—it never keeps score, never needs anything in return, and always remains generous and compassionate. In our modern culture, this idea has become increasingly alien.

There may be many other language distortion examples —enough to fill a book. Suffice it to say that our language has been assaulted, either by happenstance or intentionally.

All languages change. There are many natural forces which alter the vocabulary and the meanings of words.

What if someone wanted to eliminate the more positive meanings in our language? What if someone viewed such abilities as discrimination (discernment), responsibility, faith and love as threats to some hidden agenda? Who would think this? If we let our imaginations roam a bit, we might conjure up a criminal mastermind who wants to take over the world. But that sounds like a fantasy, doesn't it? No one would ever want that much power. No one would ever destroy the language in order to take over the world, would they?

Great Ideas Gone Wrong

Women's Liberation seemed like a great idea. Giving women the freedom to take more responsibility and to make more money for their families seemed wonderfully progressive. It meant great benefits for the families and even for single women.

In one of Aaron Russo's last interviews before his death, he revealed the details of conversations he'd had with Nick Rockefeller, supposedly of the internationally known Rockefeller family (see *Notes* in the *Appendix*). Rockefeller had told Russo that his family had funded Women's Liberation for two basic reasons: 1) to destroy the family unit and to make the children dependent upon the state, through the school system, and 2) to double the income of their private Federal Reserve banks through personal income taxes (Jones, 2009).

Many remain unfamiliar with the notion that the American Central Bank is private. The Fed controls monetary policy in the United States and creates the currency used in that country and by much of the world. Each Federal Reserve branch is owned by private banks, which are in turn owned by private individuals. Even though the Fed was created by an act of Congress, the government has no ownership of, and no control over the Fed. On numerous occasions, Fed officers have refused to reveal their inner workings to Congress, claiming that it would interfere with the Fed's independence. What crimes can be hid by such independent secrecy? If we assume that all bankers are honest and no banker has ever been greedy, then we can dismiss any concerns for Fed concealment. But is such dismissal wise?

If you are familiar with the concept of the illegal Ponzi scheme, you might recognize in the Fed's creation of currency an inevitable debt bubble. Each dollar is created with debt attached to it. This debt accumulates, grows and can never be paid off, because there is no money free of debt to extinguish the already massive burden of well over $18 Trillion. The nation's debt had nearly doubled in the second President Bush's eight years in office. And the same debt nearly doubled again in Obama's first six years in office. Like all Ponzi schemes, the Federal Reserve's currency creation method soon won't be able to sustain the weight of all that debt. Those left holding the dollars will be left out in the cold.

Saving the world for democracy also seemed like a great idea to Americans. The citizens of that great country are proud of their way of life and the freedoms afforded them by their Constitution and Bill of Rights. But perhaps they have not been proud enough, because they have given those liberties away.

When 9/11 happened, the American Congress had a law all ready to go. It was called the Patriot Act, but it was anything but patriotic. In fact, it was decidedly unpatriotic—effectively shredding portions of the American Constitution.

Since then, the United States government seemed to come up with all manner of "warm and fuzzy" sounding laws to keep their citizens feeling protected. Lurking within each of them resided a powerful time bomb of tyranny. The recently-passed "Safe and Accurate Food Labeling Act of 2015," does everything to prevent the labeling of genetically modified (GMO) foods. Confused? The names of many laws have become fraudulent—deceptively contradicting their own contents. Remember Orwell's Newspeak and doublethink?

After 9/11, whistleblowers have been demonized in the press. It seems that all of the media talk concentrated on the messenger, but almost none of it on the message. What was that message? That the government or military had committed high crimes. The whistleblowers were punished, but the criminals were never touched. Is this a repetitive accident? What are the odds against that happening?

Benjamin Franklin, one of America's founding fathers once said, "Those who would give up essential Liberty, to purchase a little temporary Safety, deserve neither Liberty nor

Safety" (*Reply to the Governor,* November 11, 1755). Increasingly, it seems that America has become the land of the slave and the home of the coward. Exceptions exist, but they seem more and more rare.

Ironically, congress persons are not allowed to read the bills upon which they are to vote. They are not given the time. Senator Rand Paul remarked in June, 2012, "Currently Congress has about a ten percent approval rate. One of the reasons is, we don't even obey our own rules. For goodness sakes. Six hundred page bill, and I got it this morning. Not one member of the Senate will read this bill before we vote on it. We're going to vote on this in the next thirty minutes. I, Senator Lee and others, will object to this. We'll have a point of order, that our own rules say that there has to be posted online for forty-eight hours. Six hundred pages. No one will read it. No wonder our approval rating is ten percent. Nobody knows what we're voting on."

Not everything is a conspiracy, granted. Sometimes other factors are at play, like accidents of timing or situation, a confluence of attitudes, or the government favorite—incompetence. But you can trace all forms of evil back to selfishness and self-concern. These have been the parents of conspiracies throughout humanity's past.

Conspiracies in History

When Brutus and his buddies got up close and personal with Julius Caesar, the great military leader was puzzled by such hatred. So many sharp knives punctured the life right out of Jules. Some time before the leader's painful demise, Brutus and his friends had conspired to end Julius Caesar's life.

Every war that was ever started was preceded by a conspiracy. The military forces did not accidentally find themselves on the battlefield, waking up swinging wildly from a bad nightmare. Usually, there was careful planning and preparation on the part of the aggressor. Every bit of their discussions was part of the conspiracy. Every bit of it was part of the premeditated murder that is war.

In January 1972, Jeb Magruder, G. Gordon Liddy, Attorney General John Mitchell and Presidential Counsel John Dean got together to discuss an illegal plan that ultimately led to the break-in at the Watergate Complex in Washington, DC. This conspiracy resulted in dozens of top government officials serving time in jail. It also resulted in the forced resignation of President Nixon.

On numerous occasions, Tiger Woods had conspired with a woman other than his wife, to do things which ultimately proved harmful to his marriage. Each instance was a separate conspiracy.

On September 11, 2001, three planes slammed into buildings, killing roughly 3,000 people. This tragedy took planning and resources. According to the news media, and the government, this conspiracy, and the crime which followed, were the work of Osama bin Laden and his band of merry al-Qaeda men. But a growing mountain of evidence points away from bin Laden and his CIA-founded, al-Qaeda organization. Even the FBI (America's Federal Bureau of Investigation) admits that they do not have enough evidence to add 9/11 to bin Laden's list of crimes. Yet the American government held for years the notion that bin Laden was the 9/11 boogie man and ultimately murdered him in his home, dumping his body in the ocean before telling anyone. With all the other lies we've heard from the American government, can we be certain it really was bin Laden?

Shortly after 9/11, the Afghani Taliban had offered to extradite bin Laden, if America could provide compelling evidence against the man. Instead of taking the easy way,

America continued bombing Afghanistan. A war could've been prevented with some simple pieces of paper, but America apparently did not have the evidence against bin Laden. Or if it did, preferred war despite the evidence. I don't know which is worse—American stupidity (going to war over something about which there was no evidence) or vile evil (going to war because they preferred war to a peaceful solution).

If not bin Laden, then who? The events of 9/11 were not accidents. Someone planned it all. At least one conspiracy had led to 9/11. That fact seems not to have been disputed by anyone. Yet, two American presidents went out of their way to caution others against all talk of "conspiracy theories." We have to wonder why? Like the theories found in science, some conspiracy theories are based on facts. And when someone doesn't want others talking about uncomfortable facts, it only looks as though they are hiding something.

How Common are Conspiracies? Dirt Ordinary?

Conspiracies are not some kooky or spooky myth, but many Americans seem to treat them that way, especially in the corporate media and frequently in the entertainment media. Terms like "conspiracy nut," "tinfoil hat," "crazy conspiracy theories" and the like, are all too common in the popular culture. Are those terms warranted? Certainly some crazy ideas exist which are based upon opinion, creativity or even delusion. Critical thinking, though, has been replaced with knee-jerk reactions. Instead of looking at the facts, mere mention of the word "conspiracy" and many Americans will look away. Your author felt that unnatural panic and, for a moment, looked away. In a very real sense, Orwellian Newspeak has arrived, because an entire topic has been made relatively invisible. But who would want people not to think of such things?

Conspiracies remain dirt ordinary. This book includes an informal study which found that at least *an average 489 new conspiracies start every second* somewhere on Earth, all year long, day-in and day-out. This rough figure—489 new conspiracies per second—is conservative. Many categories of conspiracies were not included, because there was insufficient information about them. Conspirators do not give up their information willingly. In fact, they would prefer that their conspiracies remain shrouded in darkness. That remains a trait common to all evil.

The calculations performed in this book are only meant to give us a ballpark idea. All criticism is invited. I have no doubt there will be some. I also invite other researchers to dig deeper and to come up with more rigorous numbers. For now, these numbers fulfill our need—to achieve a qualitative idea of the scope of conspiracies in our world. The purpose is to place the word "conspiracy" into its proper perspective.

Conspiracies are a part of life on this planet, because people tend to be selfish and self-concerned. It's part of human nature to want things we don't have. Frequently, we seek help from others to accomplish our goals. But it's only a conspiracy if the talk is about doing something unethical or illegal. Regrettably, these days, some laws are illegal or unethical. When laws are created that run counter to the guiding principles in a nation's constitution, the legislators who created those laws have conspired (yes, conspiracy) to skirt that constitution.

In this book, we will explore the nature of conspiracies and the growing danger from them. We will also look at some possible solutions.

Chapter 1:
Kids Will Be Kids

Have you ever wanted something so much that you thought you might go crazy waiting for it? Children seem to do this all the time.

Even though nearly half a century has passed since my own childhood, I can remember clearly the restless feelings of desire.

What happens when two or more kids get together to talk about doing something they know they shouldn't? That's a conspiracy—to breathe together *(com + spirare)*.

Conspiracy is not the actual doing of the crime; it is merely the talking about the doing with intent. One person talking to their self is not a conspiracy. It takes two or more to do this tango.

Imagine for a moment, two young brothers—5 and 7— have been left at home while their mother ran down to the store for a few minutes to get something important for dinner. The older boy saw an opportunity, but didn't want to get caught or to have his younger brother tattle on him.

"You like cookies, don't you?" asked Billy.

"Sure," said Tommy, cocking his head to the side, furrowing his brow with suspicion.

"Would you like a cookie, now?"

Tommy nodded rapidly.

Lifting his pointer finger to his lips, Billy used his other hand to wave his brother forward.

In the kitchen, Billy pulled over a chair and stood on it to reach the cookie jar on a lower shelf. Gingerly, he deposited the jar on the counter and carefully opened the lid. "Here," he said, handing Tommy one cookie. "Be careful. Don't leave any crumbs."

Billy pulled out two cookies for himself, closed the lid and placed the jar back on the shelf.

"Why do you get two?" asked Tommy.

"Well, I did the work," answered Billy. "And don't talk to mommy about this. Remember, she said not to eat cookies without her permission."

"Oh, okay."

Self-Concern—The Tree that Bears Conspiracy Fruit

The world is not going to end because two boys ate cookies their mother said they should not. But their actions included a conspiracy to disobey their mother and to hide that fact. This is a pretty lightweight conspiracy.

What's behind this dynamic? Selfishness, of course, or self-concern. One boy loved the satisfaction of eating cookies so much that he was willing to disobey his mother in order to fulfill his desire.

Naturally, he did not want to get caught. He included his younger brother so that Tommy would become an accomplice and would be far less likely to tell their mother.

Each step was based upon self-concern.

Every conspiracy follows this basic pattern.

Parents and Neighbors Setting Bad Examples

If parents say one thing and do another, they are setting bad examples for their children. Those parents are grooming hypocrites. If parents cut corners, the kids learn to do the same. Kids also learn from their neighbors and peers.

"Come on, don't be chicken. Cluck, cluck, cluck, cluck... You want this as much as I do."

Sometimes other kids will talk their friends into doing something they shouldn't in order to have help. Other times it might merely be to have emotional support—knowing that someone else is in the crime with them helps them overcome their own inhibitions.

Every unethical or illegal plan by such a group amounts to a conspiracy.

Gangs and Conspiracies

Little Alan was a shy young man. When he heard other boys talking outside his house, he opened his front door and approached them, one careful step at a time. Hot, West Texas sun bore down on his head. Within that heat, he hoped to find relief from his summer vacation boredom.

While he recognized Aubrey from school, the others remained strangers. But not for long.

The leader was named Dusty.

"We're just going to kick around, have some fun," said Dusty. "Want to join us?"

"Sure," replied Alan, feeling a tingling rush. Rarely had other boys his age ever asked him to join in their activities.

Moments later, they were all walking down the street together, like some guerilla platoon.

Several blocks later, they came to an unpaved alley.

"Hey, try this," said Dusty. "See this building?" He pointed to the one next to them, one story tall with a flat roof. "Let's see who can toss a stone onto the roof without making a sound."

Promptly, Dusty snatched up a stone from the ground and hurled it into the air. Knick-a-knick, it clattered across the unseen tar on the roof.

Each of the boys tried their hand at this new game, but every pebble they tossed made at least some noise.

"You guys are great," tittered Alan. "This is fun."

"Oh, yeah?" asked Dusty, then took Alan to the ground and pinned him.

Alan was too stunned at first to move, then struggled fiercely. He couldn't break free.

Finally, Dusty got up and brushed himself off.

Alan slowly recovered, picked himself up and looked angrily at Dusty.

"We're going to have to toughen you up," said Dusty.

"You want to join our group?" someone asked.

Alan glanced to Aubrey who grinned back easily.

Alan swallowed, then nodded.

"Well," said Dusty, "You've got to be tough. You've got to be tested."

"You ready?" asked Aubrey.

"I—I don't know what you mean." Alan's face burned. He took one small step away from them and tensed involuntarily.

"You've got to kill something," said Aubrey.

More Serious Crimes

This was not stealing cookies. The gang had befriended a shy and impressionable young man. They had started their relationship with a fun game. Then the leader had roughed him up, shaking his worldview. The gang members dangled the carrot of belonging in front of him, encouraging him to do something unthinkable in order to win his own membership—a relationship Alan had thought he had already obtained.

Now, he had to kill something, like a toad, dog or a cat.

If Alan were to stay in the group, he might next have to do something even more unethical or illegal—underage drinking or smoking, shoplifting, stealing a car, armed robbery or murder.

Alan had experienced his first taste of a gang conspiracy. He let it be his last.

How Many Child Conspiracies Per Year?

According to the World Population Clock (worldometers.info), roughly 26% of the world's population ranges from 0 to 14 years of age. Another 16.3% cover the age range from 15 to 24. Because we are interested only in rough figures, we will take half of the older range to get children from 15 to 19 years of age. Adding the percentages and multiplying by the current world population of about 7,362,346,000 (as of August 25, 2015), we derive about 2,514,241,000 children. Lacking solid information on the rates of childhood conspiracies, let us assume an extremely low figure of 0.1% (a tenth of a percent) for our number of conspiracies per year from children.

For the total number of conspiracies we are working toward, we will treat all school-related conspiracies separately.

What types of conspiracies? We've already seen one: stealing cookies. We also have sneaking out at night, stealing money, shoplifting, vandalism, animal abuse, underage drinking and smoking, illicit drug use, gang assault, gang rape and murder. There are also a number of possible conspiracies related to school, but we'll cover them in the next chapter.

Contributing to this low percentage, children under age three are not likely to be conspiring. Many cultural unknowns also make it dangerous to assume too high a percentage. Yet, there is a very real possibility that the number of childhood conspiracies remains far higher than this estimate—2,514,241 conspiracies per year. This rough figure would give us a new childhood conspiracy starting every 12.55 seconds.

Chapter 2:
Epidemic of Cheating

Starting in June, 2014 and working through March, 2015, I taught two semesters at a local college, here in the Philippines. Though it proved to be a richly rewarding experience, I was dismayed that so much cheating was occurring. In the college algebra class I taught, I discovered several dozen instances of student cheating in one semester.

The school is a small, four-year college, specializing in business, accounting, information technology, hospitality management and training for educators. Because I was hired as an information technology professor, I was keen to develop a lesson plan that supported I.T. related topics. Two of my algebra classes, however, each had a significant number of non-I.T. students. So, I had to adjust my lesson plan accordingly.

The college catered to lower-income students making higher education available to kids who might not otherwise have been able to afford the tuition. I had expected a hungrier bunch who would have applied themselves with far more zeal. Instead, I found a significant number of them resentful of the challenges I offered them. I varied my approach to the subject, hoping to reach those who were most falling behind.

To be fair, I did have many hardworking students, some of whom excelled in their coursework. I remain deeply grateful for all their efforts.

The joy of grading exams led me to two most disheartening discoveries. First, a majority of my I.T. students did very poorly. Initially, this puzzled me. Then, I did a simple analysis of my best students and found that a vast majority of them were enrolled in the business and accountancy program. This made sense; accountants already love numbers. Then, I realized that the information technology students had little or no idea what a career in computers involved. I suspected that, to them, computers were all Facebook, games and YouTube. They were receiving the rather rude awakening that a computer career involves numbers and logic.

My second surprise came when I discovered, on separate occasions, that the wrong responses on one student's answer sheet, exactly matched the wrong responses on another student's answer sheet. Having matching right answers would prove difficult to determine if cheating were involved. With matching wrong answers, the possibility that both students suffered the same delusion on more than one answer, was vanishingly small.

In a small classroom, packed with students, chances for cheating on an exam are greatly multiplied. In those classes, I would create two exams and alternate with them so that no two students were sitting next to one another with the same exam. Despite this, and despite carefully monitoring the students throughout each exam, there were a dozen instances of cheating in one classroom during the entire semester. In one instance, a student copied answers from the wrong exam.

They had exam #2 and copied answers from someone with exam #1. Oops!

I had no idea how many instances of cheating I had missed. Also, I had little idea how many of the cheats were conspired. Had one student merely looked onto another student's exam without them knowing it? Or had both students worked together to share answers? Also, on more than one occasion, I had to dismiss students who talked during an exam, despite multiple warnings beforehand.

Though this was a small college in a metropolitan area of more than a million people, I doubt if these were isolated or rare instances.

American Students

Most kids love to please their parents and loathe making them disappointed or angry. When it comes to school performance, they are no different. This becomes an especially potent force when parents offer rewards for better scholastic standing.

A poll performed in 2013 by NBC television, in America, revealed that 63% of American college students admitted to cheating. That's nearly two-thirds of all students. This survey did not reveal how many times the students had cheated in any one year. There may have been some who cheated multiple times. In the news segment, an NBC staffer played the part of a college student conspiring to have someone else write a term paper for them.

How many students work with others to accomplish their cheating? This is also unknown from the study. But let us assume that only 10% of American college student cheating involves a conspiracy—talking with at least one other person to accomplish their crime.

In 2015, Institute of Education Sciences (IES), from their National Center for Education Statistics, estimated that 20.2

million students would be going to college in the coming fall, in the United States. If the same percentage holds, then 12.7 million students will be cheating. Many of them might be solo cheaters, taking scraps of paper into their exams or writing key information or formulas on their arm or hand. Others might share answers during an exam using a cell phone or other method of communication. Some might even conspire to break in and steal exam answers from the professor's desk.

With so many students willing to cheat, it would seem likely that many would include someone else in their plans to do so. Yet, we choose a conservative figure—only 10% of all cheaters. This would give us about 1.27 million conspiracies. And, being conservative with our figures, we will assume that there is only one instance of cheating per year for each of these students.

Of course, the survey said 63% of college students admitted to cheating. We have no idea how many did not admit to cheating. So, the actual cheating percentage could be higher.

Averaged over the entire year, this gives us 2.4 new conspiracies every minute, or a new conspiracy starting every 25 seconds.

Outside American College Academia

Of course, this figure includes only college or university students in the United States. What about other American students? And what about students in other countries?

IES estimates that 50.1 million students will attend elementary and high school in 2015. That's 35.2 million pre-kindergarten through grade 8, 14.9 million in grades 9 through 12, and an additional 4.9 million in private schools.

While there may have been studies of cheating in the primary and secondary schools, those may only tell part of the story. Some cheaters may never admit to having cheated. Let us assume that pre-kindergarten through grade 8 have far lower rates of cheating and conspiracy. Arbitrarily, the figure of 1% has been chosen to represent the number of cheaters who involve one or more others in their crimes. This gives us 352,000 conspiracies in the lower grades.

For high school students, we arbitrarily choose 50% as our figure for cheating and repeat our figure of 10% of the cheating which involves one or more other individuals. The supposition here is that the older kids are more "worldly," moving toward the rates of college students. For those who already cheat, let us assume that the need to include others is roughly equal to that found in college students. This gives us another 990,000 conspiracies per year.

All totaled, this gives us a rough estimate of 1,342,000 conspiracies in American non-college schools for children.

Geoff Maslen, writing in early 2012 for University World News, said, "The number of students around the globe enrolled in higher education is forecast to more than double to 262 million by 2025." This would mean that the current level of students is roughly 131 million or slightly less. Subtracting about 20 million to account for the American part, this leaves us with about 111 million college students, internationally.

Extrapolating from the American figures to international education, we achieve rough estimates of 5,550,000 non-American college conspiracies, and 55,170,000 non-American, primary and secondary education conspiracies.

Again, these are very rough figures only meant to give us a ballpark idea. Many dynamics will affect the actual numbers—cultural differences, availability of resources and perhaps other factors.

These give us a total of 63,334,600 conspiracies per year in the standard educational system, worldwide. Cautiously taking this figure as accurate, this would mean 2.007 new conspiracies per second in grades pre-kindergarten through university level, worldwide.

We've attempted to use conservative figures, but realize that other factors may be involved which could greatly alter the numbers to be found in a more rigorous study.

Implications

There is little doubt that cheating has always been with us, as long as education has existed. Conspiracies to cheat may have existed for a large portion of that time. But was cheating always this bad?

Could the current culture be feeding this? Fast food, instant gratification, fast internet connections—fast, fast, fast. Children seem to be more impatient these days—or at least they're more open with their impatience.

Movies increasingly have made honesty, and similarly positive traits, socially unacceptable. It's cool to steal. It's okay to curse and to slander someone else. It's natural to be bad. One book series, made into movies—*The Maze Runner*—explicitly states that " WCKD [wicked] is good."

The heroes are gangsters and intelligent burglars. Mission Impossible and Jack Bauer bend the rules, but get the job done.

Why wouldn't a student want to be like their heroes?

Chapter 3:
Federal Bureau of
Incompetence or Involvement?

There is no doubt that many hard working, honest agents labor for America's Federal Bureau of Investigation (FBI). But the tone and behavior of an organization is invariably established by its leadership. When the leadership remains corrupt, it affects the entire organization. Those who do good, ethical jobs, might end up suffering for their good works.

Repeatedly, the FBI has been caught conspiring to commit terrorists acts in order to foil them.

The 1993 World Trade Center Bombing—FBI Snafu

In one of the more infamous such conspiracies—the one that led to the 1993 World Trade Center bombing—the FBI's informant had secretly taped his conversations with FBI agents. These tapes later proved to be very embarrassing to the agency.

"Two cassette tape recordings, obtained by Shadow reporter Paul DiRienzo of telephone conversations between FBI informant Emad Salem and his Bureau contacts reveal secret U.S. Government complicity in the February 26, 1993 bombing of the World Trade Center in New York City in which six people were killed and more than a thousand were injured" (Lectric Law Library).

New York Times reporter, Ralph Blumenthal, wrote, "The transcript quotes Mr. Salem as saying that he wanted to complain to F.B.I. headquarters in Washington about the bureau's failure to stop the bombing, but was dissuaded by an agent identified as John Anticev." Blumenthal added, "Mr. Salem is quoted as telling [FBI] agent Floyd: 'Since the bomb went off I feel terrible. I feel bad. I feel here is people who don't listen'."

Investigative reporter, Jon Rappoport wrote of this event, "Is there anything under the sun the FBI can be held accountable for…because letting the bomb plot go forward… what else do you need for a criminal prosecution of the Bureau?" He added, "But the role of the FBI is clear enough. They aided and abetted, and at the very least, permitted the 1993 attack on the Trade Towers."

Pre-9/11 FBI Field Excellence; Headquarters Bungling?

In the months before 9/11, individual FBI agents attempted to track and/or question terrorists known to be in the country and known to be receiving flight training.

In 2002, R. Joseph wrote for Rense.com, "In October of 1996, FBI agents in Phoenix were also informed by an under-cover agent, Harry Ellen, that a number of Arab extremists at a local mosque were receiving aviation training. Ellen was alarmed and informed the Phoenix office 'that it would be terrible if the bad guys were able to gain this kind of access to airplanes, flight training and crop dusters. You really ought to look at this, it's an interesting mix of people.'… one of the bad guys was Hanji Hajour, one of the September 11 hijackers." Joseph added, "Several of the other hijackers had also been granted visas and allowed into this country in the weeks and months before 9/11 although they were known to be veterans of previous terrorist attacks."

Joseph made even stronger statements against the FBI and the American government. "The FBI, CIA, and Bush administration, not only had advanced and detailed information and then did nothing to prevent the 9/11 assault and murder of 3000 Americans, they tried to cover it up and then lied about it.

"After the September 11, attack, Robert S. Mueller III, Director of the FBI, said he was surprised to discover there were terrorists in the U.S., and even more surprised to learn they had been receiving flight training. 'This is news to me' he said, and then added, 'obviously, if we had understood that to be the case, we would have averted this.'"

Dan Eggen and Bill Miller wrote, in May, 2002, for the *Washington Post*, "Minneapolis FBI agents investigating terror suspect Zacarias Moussaoui last August were severely hampered by officials at FBI headquarters, who resisted seeking search warrants and admonished agents for seeking help from the CIA,..."

One government official commented on FBI headquarters incompetence, saying, "There was a great deal of frustration expressed on the part of the Minneapolis office toward what they viewed as a less than aggressive attitude from headquarters. The bottom line is that headquarters was the problem."

Known terrorists were allowed to get visas into the United States, were being tracked by the FBI, and the FBI later pretended not to know.

Some of the field agents were doing their jobs; the same cannot be said of the bureau's leadership.

But the FBI was not the only agency acting in a corrupt manner. Years earlier, J. Michael Springmann, chief of the visa section at the consulate in Jeddah, Saudi Arabia, had noticed suspicious activity and did the right thing. Several young men had wanted visas to the United States, but could not answer simple questions about their reasons for traveling to America. One said he wanted to go to a trade show, but could not tell Springmann the name of the city where the trade show was to be held. After refusing several such visas, a CIA agent working at the consulate insisted that the young men be given visas. Springmann again refused. Though he did the right thing— following American law—his contract as chief of the visa section was not renewed.

Post-9/11 FBI Cover-up?

Michael Stratford, wrote for Demand Media, "The FBI to date has released only two videos recording the 9/11 attack on the Pentagon,... The FBI's speedy retrieval of the tapes is corroborated by several witnesses, among them Jose Velasquez, a gas-station supervisor whose security cameras allegedly recorded the moment of impact when Flight 77 hit the Pentagon. 'Within minutes, the FBI was there and took the film,' Velasquez told the Richmond Times Dispatch."

It seems that the FBI continues to cover up details about 9/11. Paul Sperry recently wrote in the New York Post, "Just 15 days before the 9/11 attacks, a well-connected Saudi family suddenly abandoned their luxury home in Sarasota, Fla.,... even a refrigerator full of food." Sperry added, "Neighbors took note of the troubling coincidence and called the FBI, which opened an investigation that led to the startling discovery that at least one 'family member' trained at the same flight school as some of the 9/11 hijackers in nearby Venice, Fla."

Sperry went on to write, "Former Democratic Sen. Bob Graham, who in 2002 chaired the congressional Joint Inquiry into 9/11, maintains the FBI is covering up a Saudi support cell in Sarasota for the hijackers. He says the al-Hijjis' 'urgent' pre-9/11 exit suggests 'someone may have tipped them off' about the coming attacks."

According to Sperry, Senator Graham also stated, "This is a pervasive pattern of covering up the role of Saudi Arabia in 9/11 by all of the agencies of the federal government which have access to information that might illuminate Saudi Arabia's role in 9/11."

Russ Baker, in his article for WhoWhatWhy, wrote of their interview with former Senator Graham, "Bob Graham... described a remarkable interaction with a 'very senior' FBI official around the time of the tenth anniversary of 9/11." Two FBI agents had intercepted Graham and his wife at the airport while the couple were on a trip to visit their daughter in Virginia. The FBI spent about an hour trying to convince him to leave the inquiry alone and that it was a dead end. Graham told the FBI agents of a discrepancy in their reports and asked to see the documents which clarified this. The lead agent agreed and set up a meeting for days later. When Graham arrived for the meeting, the same FBI agent told him, "Your meeting here has been canceled, is not going to be rescheduled, and incidentally, I know you've been trying to contact the agent who wrote the report, and I have told him not to talk with you."

Baker added, "We have seen similar behavior in relation to the Boston Marathon Bombing, the Oklahoma City Bombing, TWA Flight 800, and other violent incidents attributed by federal authorities to isolated renegades or some accident. And Graham is not the only investigator who has been ordered by FBI personnel to stop digging into such incidents, stop talking about them, stop asking questions."

Joshua Cook, of TruthInMedia.com, wrote, "Graham said that a smoking gun in this case [is] contained in 80,000 documents being reviewed by a federal judge in south Florida. The documents... which are being released little by little, show a connection between a wealthy Florida family, the Saudi royal family and the hijackers.

"Graham... had first hand knowledge of these documents, says that the FBI is covering up the fact that it investigated this family. Judge Andrew Napolitano told Fox News' Shepard Smith that he believes that Graham has seen the documents and knows exactly what's in them.

"Napolitano noted that President Obama signed an arms deal last year with the [Saudis] for $60 billion to provide weapons to them for the next ten years. 'It's a very dangerous stew here,' said Napolitano."

Officials of the American government don't seem to want to hear that their Saudi friends may have been involved in 9/11. Is it possible that they already know this and merely do not want this knowledge made broadly public?

Boston Bombing

Tony Cartalucci (2013) wrote for InfoWars.com, "CBS reveals in their report, 'CBS News: FBI Interviewed Tamerlan Tsarnaev 2 Years Ago,' that the FBI initially attempted to deny any contact prior to the Boston bombings with slain suspect Tamerlan Tsarnaev. It was only after Russia's RT publicly pursued the story that the FBI finally admitted officially it had." His report goes on to provide several examples of FBI plots to foster, fund and equip American terrorists.

Why did the FBI initially deny prior contact with the suspect? Was this something discussed within the agency, or did the FBI person responding make a unilateral decision to lie. If the lie was a group decision or even an executive decision passed down the chain of command, it seems to have been a clear conspiracy to lie to the press and the world.

More Hanky Panky

In another report by Tony Cartalucci (2012), he wrote, "USA Today reports that a suspect had been arrested by the FBI who was 'en route to the U.S. Capitol allegedly to detonate a suicide bomb.' While initial reports portrayed the incident as a narrowly averted terrorist attack, CBS would report that a 'high ranking source told CBS News the man was "never a real threat".' The explosives the would-be bomber carried were provided to him by the FBI during what they described as a 'lengthy and extensive operation.' The only contact the suspect had with 'Al Qaeda' was with FBI officials posing as associates of the elusive, omnipresent, bearded terror conglomerate. The FBI, much like their MI5 counterparts in England, have a propensity for recruiting likely candidates from mosques they covertly run."

Conspiracies All

Every one of these covert operations or lies by the FBI remains a probable conspiracy by government agents or agency executives. At least one such operation got out of hand and resulted in the deaths of 6 people and the injury of more than a thousand others, plus more than a billion dollars of damage to the World Trade Center—this more than 8 years before 9/11.

The government seemed to protect the 9/11 hijackers before the day of tragedy. Many times, the FBI created terrorists so that they could foil their evil plots. Would the ones arrested have become possible terrorists if the FBI had not become involved and encouraged them to participate? Likely, we'll never know. What remains clear, though, is that the FBI is conspiring to commit horrible crimes. In some cases, they are creating far more damage and loss than we can afford, but that's only for the instances about which we have clear knowledge. How many secrets is the FBI hiding?

Not including 9/11 on bin Laden's list of crimes may have been one of the few truly honest things the FBI has done as an organization. Again, there is no doubt that the bureau has many honest, hardworking people in its ranks, but the leadership does not seem so pure.

CIA Complicity?

Jeff Stein, a *Newsweek* columnist wrote, "Mark Rossini, a former FBI special agent at the center of an enduring mystery related to the September 11, 2001 terrorist attacks, says he is 'appalled' by the newly declassified statements by former CIA Director George Tenet defending the spy agency's efforts to detect and stop the plot.

"Rossini, who was assigned to the CIA's Counterterrorism Center (CTC) at the time of the attacks, has long maintained that the U.S. government has covered up secret relations between the spy agency and Saudi individuals who may have abetted the plot. Fifteen of the 19 hijackers who flew commercial airliners into the World Trade Center towers, the Pentagon, and a failed effort to crash into the U.S. Capitol, were Saudis."

Stein added, "Rossini claims still-classified documents would 'show a pattern of financial assistance, and moreover, the CIA's role to try and recruit al-Mihdhar.' He says he was 'convinced' of that and that 'there is no other explanation' for the CIA refusing to release further information....

"Rossini and his colleague, Miller, following the CTC's strict rules on secrecy, kept silent for years about their thwarted effort to warn FBI headquarters about al-Mihdhar, providing critics with ammunition to cast doubt on their story. But in a *Newsweek* interview, a former FBI colleague has now come forward publicly for the first time to buttress their version of events."

Special Agent John O'Neill—The One Who Knew

The late John P. O'Neill has been characterized as once having been the FBI's leading expert in al-Qaeda, terrorism and Osama bin Laden. After repeated attempts, O'Neill could not get the FBI to dig deeper into what he viewed as an increasing threat to America. Late in 2001, O'Neill resigned from the FBI citing repeated obstructions to his efforts to investigate al-Qaeda. He started work at the World Trade Center as head of security. He died in the building collapse on 9/11 while coordinating a rescue attempt in the upper floors of one of the towers.

O'Neill started at his new job on August 23, 2001, hired by Jerome Hauer, managing director at Kroll (Wright). O'Neill had proved to be a thorn on the subject of Osama bin Laden and al-Qaeda. If anyone in the government had wanted to get rid of him and his in-depth knowledge, dangling the carrot of a higher paying job at the World Trade Center would have been perfect. But this only makes sense if someone in the government had prior knowledge of an impending attack there.

Perhaps it should not be surprising that many facts point to such prior knowledge. That by itself could be the subject of an entire book. There were terrorism drills which included an illustration of the World Trade Center in crosshairs.

There was intelligence chatter about terrorists targeting US buildings. FBI field agents knew of known terrorists learning piloting skills which focused on take-offs, but not landings.

A story published by Ananova, November, 2001, entitled, "US agents told to back off bin Ladens," stated, "The BBC says that America's special agents backed away from the bin Laden family soon after George W Bush became president.

"Agents were also told to back off the Saudi royals— although that has all changed since September 11."

According to some sources, presidential directive W199i had prohibited John O'Neill from investigating members of the bin Laden family—making it a crime to hinder the work of Abdullah bin Laden in any way (911Myths.com, Talboo and others).

On January 17, 2002, Manhattan US Attorney, Mary Jo White, received the first award given in O'Neill's name. According to author, Murray Weiss, White "focused on the true measure of O'Neill's life: that he contributed more to recognizing and fighting terrorism than any [other] one man."

Was O'Neill killed by elements within the government for what he knew? We may never know the answer to this. There may be no conspiracy which targeted him and led to his death; but then again, there may have been.

Chapter 4:
Crimes, Crimes and
More Crimes

In August, 2015, I corresponded several times with the FBI in order to determine if they had statistics on the number of perpetrators in each crime. How many crimes had single perpetrators; and how many had multiple perpetrators? This seemed to be an important dynamic in understanding the nature of each crime. Yet, I was informed in no uncertain terms that they do not possess such statistics. I still find this too incredible to believe, but there it is.

America's FBI includes many statistics on their website. A great many of these are gathered from other law enforcement agencies in cooperation with the national agency.

What we are interested in looking at, here, are those crimes which can sometimes involve others—conspiracies.

According to FBI statistics on crimes committed in the United States, white collar crime (NIBRS data), there are 5,428,613 total incidents. This includes 4,078,106 known offenders, 2,025,419 unknown offenders, and 6,103,525 total offenders. From this, we derive 674,912 maximum known conspiracies for white collar crimes (and there may be some unknown ones).

This is for 1997–1999 and accounts for 3.8% of incidents reported to the FBI. There are an unknown number of incidents not reported to the bureau. Because this is for a range of years, we take the average—224,971 per year—and the 1998 population (middle of 3 years)—270,248,003. This gives us 0.000832, or 83.2 per 100,000 (0.083%). In other words, this yields less than a tenth of a percent as our rate for white collar crime percentage (WCC%).

For some crimes, it is estimated that the percentage of conspiracies is very low. For this "Rare" percentage we will arbitrarily use 0.001%.

Some crimes frequently require other people to be involved. Conservatively, we will use 10%. And there are a few crimes that cannot be committed without others being involved.

For the following crimes, it is estimated that all are single perpetrator events. Any exceptions are likely extremely rare or nonexistent.

- Curfew and loitering
- Vagrancy
- Disorderly conduct
- Drunkenness
- Weapons; carrying, possessing, etc.
- Rape (excluding gang rape)
    Crimes using the "Rare" percentage include,
- Those listed under "all other offenses" —3,282,651 = 33 conspiracies
- Driving under the influence—1,166,824 = 12 conspiracies
- Offenses against the family and children—101,247 = 1 conspiracy

- Sex offenses (except rape and prostitution)—57,925 = 1 conspiracy
- Miscellaneous assaults—1,097,741 = 11 conspiracies
- Aggravated assault—358,860 = 4 conspiracies
- Murder and non-negligent manslaughter—10,231 = essentially zero conspiracies.

The following crimes seem to give us greater opportunity for cooperative efforts (conspiracies). Here we conservatively use WCC%.

- Arson—10,509 = 9 conspiracies
- Motor vehicle theft—64,566 = 54 conspiracies
- Larceny-theft—1,231,580 = 1,025 conspiracies
- Burglary—252,629 = 210 conspiracies
- Robbery—94,406 = 79 conspiracies

For vandalism, we will estimate a slightly higher level of participation or gang related activity, and use 1%.

- Vandalism—201,168 = 2,012 conspiracies

The next three items are more frequently associated with others. Yet, we'll remain conservative at 10% conspiracies.

- Embezzlement—15,730 = 1,573 conspiracies
- Fraud—143,528 = 14,353 conspiracies
- Forgery and counterfeiting—60,969 = 6,097 conspiracies

Stolen property frequently requires a buyer and that constitutes a conspiracy. Even so, we will use a conservative 50% for our conspiracy rate, because some are arrested merely for possession.

- Stolen property; buying, receiving, possessing—92,691 = 46,346 conspiracies

The following crimes are set at 100% because they require both a buyer and a seller.

- Liquor laws—354,872 = 354,872 conspiracies
- Gambling—6,024 = 6,024 conspiracies

The total of all these is 432,713 conspiracies from this list of crimes. This is from the FBI's Table 29, Estimated Number of Arrests, United States, 2013. I have excluded arrests for prostitution and commercialized vice, as well as those for drug abuse violations, because these are included in the international figures, below.

This does not include the crimes committed for which arrests were not made. That could greatly increase the number of conspiracies if there were some way to determine the total number. Criminals are rarely so cooperative.

International Crimes

For the same crimes outside of the United States, we will use a conservative figure of 9,559,431 conspiracies. This may be overestimated in some respects, because not all countries have the same percentages of crimes per capita. And in some respects, this may be an underestimation for similar reasons. What we're after is merely a rough idea—a ballpark figure for the total number of conspiracies in the world. Because there are roughly 23.1 times as many people outside of America as live in that country, we use this factor times the number of American conspiracies. This gives us a total of 9,992,144 conspiracies.

From this list of conspiracies, we will average 0.317 new conspiracies per second, or a new conspiracy starting every 3.16 seconds.

Illegal Drug Use—Worldwide

According to United Nations' figures, there are approximately 162 million illegal drug users in the world. Let us assume that each of these drug users becomes involved in twenty drug purchases in any one year. This gives us 3.24 billion illegal drug purchases. Because each of these involves a buyer and a seller, this gives us 100% conspiracies, or 3.24 billion conspiracies per year.

This gives us a rather stunning figure of about 103 new conspiracies per second throughout the year.

Prostitution—Worldwide

The United Nations also estimates that there are about 40 million prostitutes working in the world. Again, because illicit commerce is involved, this provides us with another instance of 100% conspiracy. If we estimate that each works 300 days per year and performs one trick per day, that amounts to about 12 billion tricks per year.

Every conversation the prostitutes have with potential clients constitutes a conspiracy, even if the transaction is not completed. We will ignore the failed transactions in our calculations.

This proves to be the single largest category of documented conspiracies. With prostitution providing us with roughly 12 billion conspiracies per year, this amounts to 380.251 new conspiracies per second, on average.

Crime Summary

Between drugs and prostitution, we have the lion's share of our conspiracies. These provide us with 483.251 new conspiracies each second.

On a more visceral level, these provide us with a unique look at the driving force behind conspiracies—self-concern. With drugs and illicit sex, we have the uncontrollable desire for pleasure that takes over the perpetrator-victim's life.

With all of the crimes listed, we have 483.253 new conspiracies each second.

Now that we know these facts, conspiracies seem much more commonplace. Though the more violent crimes provide a great deal of suffering, conspiracies within corporations tend to generate far more torment and agony across the world.

Chapter 5:
Corporate World

Corporations have become a world unto themselves. More than ever before, they now seem to be above the law. Untouchable.

In the 2010, Academy Award-winning documentary film, *Inside Job*, narrated by Matt Damon, Wall Street corporations are portrayed as slick, cutthroat organizations capable of great corruption. When government law enforcement agencies offer them easy options, it's no wonder that corruption on Wall Street is so rampant. The bankers paid small fines—small compared to the outrageous sums they had collected from their illegal and unethical actions. And not one banker went to jail. That was in America. They were happy to pay the fines, so long as they didn't have to admit to any wrongdoing.

Iceland also suffered similar banking problems leading up to the 2008 financial crisis, but ended up letting their banks fail, and arrested those responsible. Iceland's economy has rebounded and is now growing strong. America's economy is not so steady, especially after paying corrupt bankers nearly a Trillion dollars in bailouts. The guilty got bonuses!

It's like watching a surreal nightmare where all manner of crimes are committed and everyone around them pretends that it's business as usual.

Wall Street is not the only den of iniquity. A great many other corporations, across a broad array of industries have been guilty of conspiracies not only to defraud customers, but to lie about safety and efficacy of their products.

Statistics of conspiracies within corporations remain even harder to come by. But one thing remains certain: each corporate conspiracy packs a far more potent punch of sheer destruction than any small, street crime conspiracy.

Fiduciary Duty

Corporate officers have a fiduciary duty to improve the bottom line—the financial well-being of their corporation. If they do not live up to that responsibility, they may be guilty of a crime. At the very least, they will likely lose their jobs for nonperformance.

If a corporate executive can bend the rules or even break a few laws, yet make the corporation vastly more wealthy, then their star in the boardroom will shine very brightly indeed. This is especially the case if the fines the corporation is required to pay remain far smaller than the amount of income they are able to rake in. There is very little incentive to play by the rules; and very large incentives to break as many rules as they can get away with.

This "bottom line" mentality makes for very selfish behavior. Any positive image held by the public is merely for show. If such an image can help the bottom line, then they will lie to achieve that extra margin of corporate growth.

Does this sound cynical? How much of this is true for every corporation?

While there is little doubt that there remain exceptions to this rule of thumb, it would prove naive and foolish to consider that it never happens. After all, it remains the fiduciary duty of all corporate officers to do whatever they can to increase the corporate bottom line. If all corporations were to play by the rules, one new kid on the block who is willing to break every rule will get ahead of the others. The fact that federal law enforcement has proven to be impotent in the most egregious cases supports the notion that such corruption is rampant.

To expect foxes to behave themselves in the hen house is laughably insane.

When the largest cases against corporations were destroyed in the 9/11 collapse of World Trade Center 7, those companies and their officers effectively got off scot-free. Looks like there were a lot of winners on that day.

In recent years, this has included such things as rushing product approval through the government agency regulating their industry. It also has included a revolving door where corporate officers retire with handsome bonuses before joining the government agency which had held regulatory control over their jobs in the corporate sector. And this revolving door swings both ways. When government agency executives finish out their terms, they frequently go to work in the very industries they had regulated.

If you think this poses a great danger for conflicts of interest, you would be right. More foxes and a rapidly shrinking population of hens.

It only takes one corporate conspiracy to result in the deaths of millions. Take your pick of industries. Naturally, a car manufacturer would have to have a very popular model that suddenly blows up. This hasn't happened, but the Ford Pinto is a prime example of corporate attitudes driving a lack of safety. VP at Ford, Lee Iacocca, had not wanted to hear about safety problems. No conspiracy here. Self-concern took the front seat, while concern for customers took the back seat (Bazerman).

Big Pharma (the pharmaceutical giants) also have been found guilty of conspiring—rushing drugs to market which proved to be dangerous. The corporations paid fines, but no one went to jail over the deaths they had caused.

Killing with anger seems jail-worthy; killing with greed seems praise-worthy. Am I mistaken, or does something about this seem horribly wrong?

Erin Brockovich and PG&E

In 1993, Erin Brockovich investigated a cluster of illnesses and rallied a neighborhood in Hinkley, California to file a class action lawsuit against Pacific Gas and Electric (PG&E) for contaminating the ground water near the people's homes. A former employee came forward with a stack of documents he had been ordered to destroy. In that group of papers, a memo from 1966 revealed that corporate headquarters had known that the water had been contaminated with hexavalent chromium. It also revealed that PG&E executives did nothing about the contamination and advised their operation at Hinkley to keep secret the contamination. This conspiracy had resulted in several deaths and hundreds of serious illnesses—many of them cancers. The binding arbitration judge ordered PG&E to pay $333 million. This amount was to be distributed amongst the plaintiffs.

One university professor in Loma Linda, California, has attempted for nearly twenty years to discredit the Brockovich case. John Morgan has not been shy about his claims that the supposed cancer cluster in Hinkley was "pure fiction."

David Heath, writing for Mother Jones, is more than a little critical of Morgan's work. He writes, "But a review by the Center for Public Integrity found glaring weaknesses in Morgan's analysis that challenge the validity of his findings. In his first study, he dismisses what others see as a genuine cancer cluster in Hinkley. In his latest analysis, he excludes people who were exposed to the worst contamination."

Heath adds, "In his 2011 update, Morgan reports fewer cancers than expected in Hinkley. But he starts counting cancers in 1996, coincidentally the year PG&E settled the Brockovich lawsuit." Those who won the lawsuit moved out of Hinkley. Because the cluster no longer lived there, Morgan's updated results are meaningless—like trying to count the chickens after they had flown the coop.

PG&E had conspired to hide the dangers, pay off the families to keep them quiet, but to persist in endangering the lives of others. They wanted to cut costs. They were self-concerned. They were selfish. Were they so self-concerned that they would hire a university professor to slander the Hinkley results? If so, then that would also have been a conspiracy.

More Corporate Scandals

In the 1990s, the Internet seemed like the new Gold Rush. Investors were going crazy backing one company after another. Investment banks had promoted new Internet companies which they knew were certain to fail. This resulted in the Internet Stock Bubble of March 2000, with investors losing $5 Trillion. Every one of those frauds was a conspiracy.

After the Internet Bubble, trouble brewed on Wall Street because investment banks were bundling toxic assets and selling them as AAA-rated instrument. In other words, they lied. The rating agencies also lied by giving such high ratings. Everyone involved but the investors made lots of money. All of that fraud caught up with them with the Housing Bubble crash of 2008. So many conspiracies!

Enron was another corporation to be racked by unethical practices, many of which were conspiracies to defraud stock-holders and board members. In 2001, the failure of Enron was, up to that time, the largest corporate bankruptcy ever. Stock had plummeted from $90.75 per share to less than $1 in less than six months. Arthur Andersen, the world's largest accountancy firm was also destroyed by the their complicity in the accounting fraud, including conspiracy to shred docu-ments needed in the Enron case.

Citibank, JP Morgan and Merrill Lynch helped Enron conceal fraud. They were fined $385 million and served no jail time. They did not even have to admit to any wrongdoing (Ferguson).

WorldCom, once America's second-largest long dis-tance telephone company, was also racked by accounting scandal in 2002 and filed for bankruptcy.

In 2008, Lehman Brothers—once the fourth largest investment bank in America—had also used shady accounting practices to hide their losses from investors. The collapse of Lehman Brothers triggered a system-wide meltdown that resulted in numerous bankruptcies, unprecedented levels of foreclosures and the paralyzing of the global financial system.

For the bankers' crimes, Fed chairman Ben Bernanke and Treasury Secretary Paulson requested from Congress a $700 billion bailout. Corrupt executives, who had carefully picked their board members, received bonuses from the bailout money, enraging many Americans.

More Numbers

Corporations are likely more sophisticated than most, if not all, neighborhood gangs. They have far more resources to manage their public image and to perform stealth operations without getting caught. This is not to say that all corporations do this. Maybe some don't. In a world where performance is measured mercilessly, it would be hard to imagine corporate officers not tempted to give in to the pressure and to cut corners and to break laws. As many times as corporate officers have committed crimes and not gone to jail, it seems clear that the incentives not to do criminal acts is missing. Destroy the economy, break hundreds of laws, serve zero jail time and get millions of dollars in bonuses? Psychopaths would love this; they know the difference between right and wrong, but they don't care.

I suspect that most of us wouldn't dream of living such a corrupt lifestyle. But flies are drawn to garbage. Psychopaths are drawn to corrupt power.

It would prove to be the height of naiveté to think that this never happens. The big question is really one of degree. How much of this happens?

We may never know the full extent of corporate conspiracies. But, as we've seen, corporate conspiracies can cause far reaching damage.

Perhaps the most egregious conspiracies involve corporations which produce products that directly affect our health.

Chapter 6:
Maintaining Disease

Over a hundred years ago, most doctors cared about the health of their patients. They used natural medicines that helped the body heal itself, by providing the nutrients that strengthened the body's own immune system.

Today, many doctors think they are doing the same thing, but in effect, they are only maintaining the diseases they are treating. True health is not their concern. They don't know the history of the changes in medicine. They don't know, for instance, that many of the diseases supposedly "cured" by vaccines were almost gone when the individual vaccines were introduced. Many of those health professionals don't know that the toxins found in modern petrochemical medicines frequently kill the patient along with the disease. They don't know that the Rockefeller family, rich with oil money, invested in medical schools which adopted petrochemical pharmaceuticals, instead of more natural healing methods. If you smell "conflict of interest," here, they you've been paying attention.

Natural medicines help to strengthen the body so that its own natural defenses can fight off an illness.

In today's world, though, we no longer have health restoration—we have disease maintenance. The latter makes more money. If you cure a patient, they go home and you may never see them again. If you maintain their disease, then you will see them for the rest of their lives. *Ka-ching!*

The doctors benefit, because they get more billable visits. The pharmaceutical companies benefit, because they sell more of their drugs. The retailers benefit, because they get a piece of that pie.

People are living longer, but enjoying it less. Something is not quite right with this picture. The longevity may owe far less to the medicines than the better sanitation, clean water and more plentiful food. In modern societies without petrochemical medicines and packaging, cancer rates are far, far lower.

Throughout most of my life, doctors seemed caring and attentive. In the 1990s and later, things changed. Doctors seemed to become more and more distant and callous. Why the transformation?

Hitting Too Close to Home

A little over ten years ago, my youngest brother, Ken, went to the hospital to get some outpatient surgery on his nasal passage. It was supposed to be a minor procedure, but he almost died on the operating table. When I got to the hospital, his wife and children were surrounding his bed, but his body seemed empty of life. Ken was awake, but could barely hold a conversation. He had severe problems remembering things. He couldn't form complete sentences. He seemed like someone with an IQ of about 60. For weeks he was this way, bit by bit getting better. Eventually, after several months, he had returned to his usual, super genius IQ of 200+. (Yes, when he took an IQ test at age 14, his score was so far above 200, the assessment was marked "untestable.")

The hospital would not talk about what had happened. They had closed ranks to protect the guilty. As far as I know, the family never found out what the hospital had done wrong.

How many cases are there of medical malpractice? How many such incidents go unreported, because of hospital staffers going selfish or self-concerned? How many times have nurses and doctors talked with administrators and decided not to say anything to their patients? Every time they talk together about not doing what is right for the patient, they are guilty of conspiracy.

A friend of mine in Los Angeles had undergone minor surgery on her shoulder, but something went wrong. Afterward, she had no feeling in her arm. She found out later from another doctor that her problem could've been fixed, if it had been addressed immediately. If the hospital had admitted their mistake, they could've corrected it, but their unwillingness to expose themselves to a lawsuit made them wait too long to do anything to repair the damage. When hospital employees talk about not doing the right thing, in a case like this, they are guilty of a conspiracy.

America is such a litigious society, it's no wonder hospitals and doctors are reticent to talk openly about what they've done. They don't want to be sued. This by itself is enough to make some clam up. Unilateral decisions not to talk do not constitute a conspiracy, because it takes two or more people talking together to form a conspiracy.

Frequently though, decisions at a hospital are not unilateral. Discussions are made which weigh the pros and cons. Put this way, it sounds rather heartless. Perhaps that's the problem. Medicine used to be more compassionate. Certainly, there have always been selfish doctors, but now the administration of medicine seems to condone and reinforce a lack of compassion.

But what constitutes communication? A tilt of the head, a frown and shaking the head when another person starts to speak. All of these are communications conspiring to hide information. When the other person acquiesces, they have given tacit agreement to cooperate with the crime or unethical act.

Medical Malpractice

Many American doctors have been caught taking perks from large pharmaceutical companies to go off-label—to use their drugs for a purpose other than that approved by the Food and Drug Administration (FDA). Here we will estimate that about half of the more than a million US doctors have been involved in this practice. Each instance is a separate conspiracy, but we will estimate than only one such conspiracy occurs per year per doctor involved. This would give us 505,806 off-label conspiracies per year in America.

Because of the lack of easy information on this, we will use a conservative figure of 505,806 for the rest of the world for this off-label problem.

According to NumberOf.net, there are between 15,000 and 19,000 malpractice lawsuits filed each year. We will use the middle of this range—17,000.

Civil Justice Resource Group states that medical records report only about one fourth of all of the injuries and deaths attributable to medical malpractice in hospitals. The percentage of victims of malpractice who actually file claims is about 2.9%, based on medical records.

From these figures, we calculate that there are about 586,207 estimated yearly victims of malpractice reported (17,000/0.029). Multiplying this figure by 4, we get 2,344,828 total malpractice victims, reported and unreported. Subtracting the reported victims, we get 1,758,621 unreported victims. We will use 100% of these as conspiracies not to report. This is a rough estimate, but we will have to acknowledge that some decisions not to report may have been solitary decisions.

Using America as an average, simply because we do not have more exact figures, we find that international malpractice conspiracies might be approximately 38,851,193.

Combining all these figures, we find 1.32 new conspiracies per second from medical malpractice and off-label prescription drug use.

Abortions

According to the World Health Organization, there are between 40–50 million abortions per year. Each one of these includes a conspiracy to commit murder. There may be many more conspiracies where the abortions are never carried out. For our purposes, we will use the lower end of these figures. Because each abortion involves two or more people, 100% of them involve conspiracies.

But murder? Isn't abortion legal in America? Sadly, it is. But if you look at the definition of murder, we have a living, human being killed for no other reason than it proved to be an inconvenience to the mother. Does this sound selfish? It should.

Because the vast majority of these cases involves no medical risk to the mother for keeping the baby, we will refer to all of them as conspiracies to commit a crime.

For those who approve of abortion, we have to look at the fact that they are cheapening the very meaning of life. And when someone in government thinks that those who approve of abortion are also an inconvenience, they may be next to be murdered through some new law.

For abortions, this results in another 1.268 conspiracies per second.

Chapter 7:
Skeptical Until it Pays

Many of us look up to scientists. These educated researchers have superior reasoning and knowledge that make them admirable. They can do and think things that mere mortals don't understand.

But what if you found out that some scientists have cheated—fudged their numbers in order to please their bosses? It's happening. And such scientific cheating is happening at an alarming rate.

Fanelli reported in her study on the subject, "In surveys asking about the behaviour of colleagues,..." respondents reported on the rate of observed wrongdoing, that there were "...up to 72% for other questionable research practices."

Because a large percentage of scientific papers remain collaborative works, a similarly large percentage of fraud and other questionable practices will involve conspiracies. Arbitrarily, we will set the number of conspiracies at 50% of the total number of questionable research practices. Many scientists involved in such dubious work will likely do this more than once. However, we will set the number of such conspiracies at one per year for each scientist involved.

UNESCO estimated that there were 7,209,700 researchers in the world in 2007. We will use this as our base for computation.

Our rough calculations show that there might be around 2,595,492 scientific conspiracies per year, or another conspiracy every 12.16 seconds.

Corporate Pressure to Perform

Corporate officers likely know not to say explicitly for a scientist to bend the numbers. But when a scientist doesn't give the results needed by their funding source, the scientist soon learns of their displeasure. At the very least, the scientist is not invited to do any more work for them or to lecture for them.

But we have to ask, do the more greedy scientists talk more openly with their corporate handlers about the fraud they are committing? Each instance might constitute another conspiracy.

As we've seen, though, even non-verbal communication can constitute a harmful conspiracy.

Frequently, there is no explicit conspiracy. A corporate representative merely makes a suggestion that a researcher may be wrong. The conspiracy is in the subtext—the implication. *Either you give us the results we want, or you will not receive funding from us ever again.* Though this is not explicitly stated, the results are the same. More and more, scientists are giving in to the seduction of corporate funds. They are becoming prostitutes in white coats—laboratory minions of evil. That millions of people may suffer because of their own lack of ethical behavior does not seem to faze them. To this degree, these scientists have become psychopaths.

Corrupt CDC

One major exception occurred in August, 2014, in the United States. Dr. William Thompson, a researcher with the CDC (Centers for Disease Control) confessed to an independent researcher that he had lied to the world about a link between MMR vaccines and autism. MMR means the combination of measles, mumps and rubella vaccines into one shot. He had been part of a group of CDC researchers who had decided to trash some of their information. The CDC had lied and then sat on this critical health information for more than a decade. Because of their lies, hundreds of parents immediately lost their cases in national vaccine court. Because of their lies, millions of babies' lives were jeopardized. Many deaths may have resulted directly from their crimes.

The former head of the CDC had refused to entertain Thompson's initial concerns. Not long afterward, she had left the agency and had gone to work for Merck—a major manufacturer of the MMR vaccine. Could her decision not to investigate the problem further have been influenced by her chances at a well-paying job?

This is not the first time the CDC felt the heat of shame for criminal actions. In 1972, the CDC shut down a forty year experiment of giving syphilis to African-American men living in Tuskegee, Alabama. They had refused to give the men medicine. When those poor men died, the agency's scientists performed ghoulish autopsies to complete their experimentation.

When a government agency remains unethical and individual administrators look out for their own self-interests, instead of the good of the people they are supposed to be serving, we all lose.

Stellar Cases of Scientific Fraud

The corruption of science has been ongoing for over half a century. In some respects, it may well have started over a century ago.

When Albert Einstein submitted a paper to an editor for them to review, the famous physicist became outraged that the editor had given the same paper to another scientist to critique. This was Einstein's first and only taste of the new peer review process. With peer review, science could be censored. Only those who played by the rules would ever get published. Those who disagreed would be left out in the cold, no matter how good their data was, thus skepticism would become muzzled. Conspiracy? Perhaps there may have been a conspiracy by those who designed the peer review process. And there may also be conspiracies today by cozy groups of peer reviewers who scratch each others' backs.

NIST, 9/11 and World Trade Center 7

Three buildings in New York collapsed on 9/11. Two were hit by airplanes; one was not.

Never before—and never again, since then—has a steel frame building collapsed in on itself from office fires or airplane collisions. At the end of World War Two, an airplane crashed into the Empire State Building in New York City. There was significant damage, but the building did not suffer a collapse.

Other buildings have suffered structural failures, but when the top portions of those buildings collided with the lower portions across the region of weakness, the top portion either bounced as a whole unit, toppling to the side, or pancaked, leaving a stack of concrete slabs. Never did those buildings pulverize all of the concrete as we saw on 9/11.

The three building collapses on 9/11 were wholly unique. Instead of the top portion of each tower collapsing across the floors of airplane impact damage and toppling off to the side, each top started collapsing in on itself before the lower portion became damaged! That's like a subcompact car hitting a semi truck, the car collapsing to half its length before causing any damage to the truck. Then, when the car is completely gone, the truck is quickly demolished.

As each tower collapsed, most of its mass was ejected laterally. All of that mass was not available to help crush the increasingly stronger structure below.

A more puzzling collapse occurred hours after the destruction of the twin towers. At 5:20 in the afternoon, nearly half an hour after the BBC had announced its destruction, WTC7 fell straight down through the path of greatest resistance. This is like chopping down a tree on the side, and witnessing it fall straight down through its trunk, disintegrating into a pile of wood chips. That's not how nature works. Crushing the structure of the tree trunk requires extreme amounts of energy and the weight of the tree is insufficient to do this work. That's why the tree falls over to the side.

The most puzzling aspect of this collapse is that WTC7 fell at perfect free fall for the first eight floors of collapse. Why is this strange? Because free fall means that there was zero resistance to the collapse. And nowhere in this universe has solid steel ever offered zero resistance.

Think about this for a minute. Imagine ramming your fist through a solid steel beam and suffering no injuries. If this could ever happen, why then would anyone ever build a structure out of this substance?

This is one brazen fact that America's bureau of standards—NIST—seems to have overlooked. Either the scientists at NIST were thoroughly incompetent, or they were attempting to hide something.

When we dig a little deeper, we find that NIST scientists, in their original draft of the WTC7 report, started their timer artificially early and took the average rate of acceleration. That's fraudulent!

Imagine that you want to find the average velocity of a race car in the first few seconds of a race. You start your stopwatch. Ten seconds later, the gun goes off and the race cars lunge forward. See? All that time at zero velocity is going to mess up your measurement. That's called drylabbing. [drylabbing *n*. The act of supplying fictional yet plausible results in lieu of performing an assigned experiment.] It's cheating. And in this instance, it's supplying results that are "plausible" only if no one is paying close attention.

NIST scientists conspired to commit scientific fraud. But why?

If they had admitted to perfect free fall and its implications, they would have to admit that some other force had weakened the building—not just a little. Some other force had removed all resistance from the steel beams. Only controlled demolition can do this so that a building falls smoothly through eight floors while picking up speed at the acceleration of gravity.

Dr. Andrew Wakefield, Autism and MMR Vaccines

In a 1998 paper produced by Dr. Andrew Wakefield and nearly a dozen other researchers, claims were made that linked the MMR (measles, mumps and rubella) vaccine to autism and bowel disease. After that report was published in *The Lancet*—a British medical journal—allegations of fraud and conflicts of interest were leveled against Wakefield. The doctor lost his license to practice medicine in the UK.

Since then, Wakefield moved to the United States and has continued to push for vaccine reform and more research.

In 2012, one of the report's co-authors, Prof. John Walker Smith, won an appeal against the UK's General Medical Council (GMC). The court condemned the GMC for their sloppy work. Smith's insurance covered the expensive appeal process, but Wakefield's insurance did not. The cost of Wakefield's appeal was estimated at over $100,000. Though this ruling did not vindicate the study or Wakefield, it reveals flaws in the very system that attacked Wakefield and his work. Was Wakefield guilty of the things for which he was accused?

As mentioned earlier, a government agency knew Wakefield was right, but sat on the information. In late 2014, a CDC (Centers for Disease Control) senior scientist named Dr. William Thompson, became a whistleblower admitting that his agency had covered up their own verification of a link between MMR vaccines and autism.

We have no way of knowing how many conspiracies were committed by government agencies both in England and America, by pharmaceutical companies and by enterprising reporters who may have been a little too creative with their facts.

How many children died because of MMR vaccines between the CDC's discovery and Thompson's admission of guilt? How many children suffered autism or other damage to their health in the decade after Thompson's study was published? If Thompson and his fellow CDC scientists had been more honest, would Dr. Wakefield have been able to reclaim his license and his career. We may never know. Too many selfish interests are involved.

The media portrays Wakefield as anti-vaccine, but Wakefield himself denies this. He has merely pushed for changing the way vaccines are given and the schedule upon which they are delivered to children. If anything, this is pro-vaccine. But the media and public have made up their minds. Wakefield is guilty until proven innocent.

Wakefield commented on his relationship with the media, stating that they have "sold out." In an article by Anne Dachel, he is quoted, "I sat once with Sharyl Attkisson, one of this country's greatest journalists, working for CBS. And she said to me, 'Andy, when we finish this interview,... I will get a call from the top floor, from the money men, and they will say, that interview does not go out, because I've had a call from our pharmaceutical industry sponsors, and if it goes out, then they are going to pull their sponsorship.' And that is why she left [CBS]."

Every time the top executives of a media outlet discuss quashing a story because it might offend advertisers, they are conspiring to censor the news. This is not illegal, but it remains highly unethical. When the news itself could help save lives by changing the social dialog on a topic, not to report that news indirectly contributes to the deaths of many.

You may as well give a gun to CBS and have them slaughter thousands directly. It would prove to be more honest than hiding their culpability in their executive offices.

Science by Consensus, Settled Science, Climate Change and Climate-Gate

NASA's own website includes the words "scientific consensus." This is incredibly unscientific and highly political. Science is never, ever done by consensus. To claim this remains an *argumentum ad populum*—an argument to popularity —type logical fallacy. Science is *not* a popularity contest.

The words "scientific consensus" are popular in the media and by some government officials, but it remains junk science.

NASA also states, *"Multiple studies published in peer-reviewed scientific journals show that 97 percent or more of actively publishing climate scientists agree: Climate-warming trends over the past century are very likely due to human activities."*

The most widely quoted study on this consensus reveals the political nature of this consensus in its first sentence: "An accurate perception of the degree of scientific consensus is an essential element to public support for climate policy" (Cook). Again, this is politics; not science.

Cook, *et al*, state that the purpose of their survey was, "...to determine the level of scientific consensus that human activity is very likely causing most of the current GW (anthropogenic global warming, or AGW)."

This said nothing about global warming for the last century. NASA was overstating the case presented by Cook. *Oops!*

In Cook's own paper, he shows that 66.4% of the papers surveyed contained no explicit position on AGW. He bases his 97.1% on the percentage of those who state a position on the AGW question. So, when President Obama sends a message through Twitter,

"Ninety-seven percent of scientists agree: #climate change is real, man-made and dangerous."

He's making a *false statement*. Yet, should we really be surprised that a politician lies?

This is not 97% of all scientists, going by Cook's own numbers, this is only 97% of the 33.6% who voiced an explicit opinion. And Obama's statement contains other, quite massive flaws.

The term "climate change" has two different meanings. Scientists use it to mean cooling, warming, fast, slow, steep and shallow changes in the average global climate. The president, news media and IPCC (UN's Intergovernmental Panel on Climate Change) use "climate change" to mean strictly and only Catastrophic Anthropogenic Global Warming (CAGW)—man made dangerous warming.

I seriously think 100% of all scientists would agree that "climate change" (scientific definition) is real. Climate has changed ever since Earth gained an atmosphere, nearly 4.5 billion years ago. Climate cannot help but change. That is its nature. Climate has warmed, cooled, warmed and cooled again. Climate warming and cooling have changed slowly, quickly, over short periods and over long periods. Nearly all possible combinations of changes have been made.

It remains clear from Cook's study that only 32.6% of all scientists agree with the AGW position. But that study said nothing about CAGW (Obama's "dangerous").

Worst of all, Cook's study remains heavily flawed. A new peer reviewed paper by Dr. David Legates, *et al*, takes apart Cook's methods and data. Anthony Watts (2013), writing about Legates' work, comments, "The consensus Cook considered was the standard definition: that Man had caused most post-1950 warming. Even on this weaker definition the true consensus among published scientific papers is now demonstrated to be not 97.1%, as Cook had claimed, but only 0.3%."

Dr. Legates commented, "It is astonishing that any journal could have published a paper claiming a 97% climate consensus when on the authors' own analysis the true consensus was well below 1%."

Who put up NASA's website on scientific consensus? Were they scientifically and logically incompetent? Or did they have a meeting to discuss the pros and cons of becoming a political agency, instead of a scientific one? We don't know if any conspiracies were involved, here. If there was no conspiracy, then there has been a great deal of stupidity and incompetence involved, not only by politicians, but also by scientists and the administrators of the once "scientific" agency called NASA.

This breaks my heart. I have been biased in favor of NASA ever since the agency was founded. To see them abandon science on this topic remains one of the low points in my 65 years. But they are part of the government. To expect that they would remain unbiased and non-political remains nothing more than wishful thinking. Oh well!

NASA also writes on their "consensus" page, "Observations throughout the world make it clear that climate change is occurring, and rigorous scientific research demonstrates that the greenhouse gases emitted by human activities are the primary driver."

This statement is crazy. It's like stating that "observations throughout the world make it clear that air exists." So? The lie behind the term "climate change" is that real scientists use it to mean one thing, but this political verbiage uses a completely different definition—that of CAGW, or dangerous man made warming.

On the website of Dr. Roy Spencer, two climate scientists —Spencer and Dr. John Christy—produce a graph showing NASA satellite data of global average temperature since 1979. That graph is kept up-to-date on a monthly basis. It shows that there has been a non-warming trend for the last 17+ years.

The graph on NASA's consensus page shows ground-based data, instead of satellite data. This remains curious for a space agency, but it would not be so bad, except that the ground data is tainted. Calibration is inconsistent throughout the network of climate reporting stations. Many stations have stopped reporting, but NASA scientists have continued to include fudged data by in-filling what they think the quantities should be. One station was found to be placed in an abnormally hot location—a university campus parking lot, right above black asphalt in the Arizona sun (Watts, 2015)! Some were placed near air conditioning exhaust vents. And scores of others exist amongst airport runways and all that hot jet engine exhaust. Such poor siting makes use of loads of artificial heating which does not represent the current state of the climate.

Besides corrupt climate data from ground-based monitoring stations, government agencies have also relied on fraudulent data from climate research units. The most infamous of these was the CRU at East Anglia, made notorious by the 2009 Climate-Gate emails. In those emails, the scientists talked about fudging data, making the data achieve a desired effect to promote CAGW, and destroying data to prevent it from falling into the hands of those who might be critical of their methods. Conspiracy, conspiracy, conspiracy. Though some have claimed that the Climate-Gate scientists have been cleared of all wrongdoing, it remains clear to any non-biased individual who knows how science is done that the Climate-Gate scientists were guilty of wrongdoing. Any amount of whitewashing will not change that. Sharing data is part of the scientific process to ensure that all research is done properly and that results can be replicated. When scientists attempt to hide their data or destroy that data, they become anti-science. It seems obvious that the group that "cleared" the East Anglia scientists were themselves either incompetent or corrupt.

Throughout all of this controversy, one burning fact has *not* been broached by the media, the IPCC or government agencies. This is the fact that we reside in an Ice Age, yet the United Nations and the globalists are promoting global cooling to cure Earth's "fever." That's like dunking a hypothermia (severe cold) victim into a bath of ice water—freezing them to cure them of extreme chills. Crazy!

It would seem that the people promoting these policies are either incompetent or corrupt.

We've been in an Ice Age for 2.6 million years—ever since Earth gained those "little" white spots at the poles. The current interglacial—the Holocene—is only a geologically brief respite from the frigid climate. How brief? Climate scientist, Wallace Broecker, discussed the lengths of interglacials, stating, "...the periods of extreme warmth appear to be roughly one half of a precession cycle (i.e., ~11,000 yr) in duration."

Estimates on the length of our current interglacial period, range from 11,500–17,000 years long, depending on whether or not you include the brief warming spike before the Younger Dryas "Big Freeze." Even using the shortest of these estimates, we are already past the average interglacial length in the current Ice Age. This means that we could start our return to glacial conditions at any time. Paleoclimate records reveal that our world has experienced an accelerated cooling trend for the last 3,000 years, ever since the Minoan Warm Period. Though many interglacials have transitioned slowly back to a glacial climate—taking 4,000 to 6,000 years—some have returned to colder temperatures in a matter of centuries. But could current efforts by governments to cool down the world speed up this process to less than a century?

What would this mean? In one person's lifetime, we could go from the current warmth to frozen climate. Permanent winter could eventually extend as far south as Kansas and cover all of Northern Europe. All of that extra cold means far less rain and far greater thermal potential between the poles and equator. This potential refers to the power to create strong storms.

Are all of the UN's climate scientists ignorant of these facts? I suspect that many are not.

When Dr. John Christy was a lead author for the UN's IPCC report in 2000, he noticed a clear bias by many of his fellow scientists. In fact, during a lunch he had with some of those scientists, they discussed how to bend the numbers to achieve a far more dramatic effect in support of CAGW—dangerous man made warming. He couldn't believe what he was hearing—scientists openly conspiring to commit scientific fraud.

Chapter 8:
Of the People, By the People, and For the People
No More

The number of employees working for the NSA (National Security Agency; AKA No Such Agency) is classified, but some estimates have been quoted. We will use the low end of the estimate range—30,000. Let us assume that half of these employees work on illegal surveillance operations. Let us also assume that each of these 15,000 have an average of 10 conversations a day about these illegal operations (illegal, because they go against the Constitution's Bill of Rights). And let us also assume that they work an average of 246 days per year. This gives us 18,428,571 NSA conspiracies per year. This would give us a new conspiracy every 1.71 seconds.

With government agencies, the number of conspiracies do not matter nearly as much as the nature and reach of each conspiracy. Some government conspiracies might not prove to be deadly; they may only restrict the rights of certain individuals or of all citizens. For instance, the federal government's order to round up all Japanese Americans after Pearl Harbor was at least one conspiracy that abused the rights of roughly 70,000 American citizens. President Franklin Roosevelt was politically corrupt to betray his own citizens and to betray the Constitution he swore to defend. A commission in 1980 found little evidence of Japanese-American disloyalty. Ironically, there was not a similar round up of German-American or Italian-American citizens, though it did include a small number of resident aliens from those two countries.

According to the 2000 census, German-Americans make up 15.2% of the population. Italian-Americans make up 5.6% (Census). If these figures were roughly the same in 1942, then of the 132,165,129 population (1940), there would have been roughly 20,089,100 German-Americans and 7,401,247 Italian-Americans, for a total of 27,490,347 who might have shared internment with the Japanese-Americans, had President Roosevelt applied his criminal logic evenly.

Every conversation President Roosevelt had about implementing this internment was a conspiracy. Every conversation held by others in implementing this was also a conspiracy, including those conversations held in the Census Bureau in tracking down the location of Japanese-Americans. Every person who contributed to the rounding up and internment of these citizens was also a party to the crime, and every conversation they had on this matter was also a conspiracy.

Corrupt FDA

When America's Food and Drug Administration is staffed with former employees of food and drug companies, there remains a heightened likelihood that conflicts of interest may be involved in their day-to-day decisions. Every time those government employees have discussions which include bending their own rules to approve a product, they are committing a conspiracy.

On many occasions, the FDA has approved drugs for market, sometimes rushing the process so that the corporations will not have to spend millions and months to test their product thoroughly. Too many times, drugs have had to be recalled because the death toll grew too high. Instead of testing in the laboratory, the corporations desired to test them in the marketplace. Their bean counters decided that the deaths of thousands was an acceptable risk. Who are they to make such decisions affecting the lives of potentially millions? The FDA, with their administrators (former corporate officers), remain complicit in those deaths.

Cancer Cures Suppressed by Selfish Medical Industry?

The World Health Organization reports that there were about 8.2 million cancer deaths worldwide in 2012.

Since the early 1900s, there have been several cancer cures that were subsequently suppressed by the American Medical Association (AMA) and the FDA. The efficacy of these cures is attested by their continued popularity and the thousands of testimonials. Rather than test these so-called cures, the medical powers had law enforcement in the United States force the closure of cancer treatment centers because those methods had not been approved by the medical establishment. No rigorous tests were performed. Healing was made illegal simply because the methods had not been tested and approved. Yet, the medical establishment was unwilling to do either of these actions. Why? The most obvious possibility is that cures don't make the money that perpetual treatment does. Like America's War on Terror, a guaranteed and never-ending source of income is desirable to the big corporations. "Let them die! We'll keep them sick long enough to make $Billions."

The same people who own the big pharmaceutical companies also own the news media. Their former employees work in the FDA and AMA. Conspiracy? Potentially, there are lots of conspiracies involved in this multi-billion dollar industry. If a petty thief can kill for pocket change, how many people would an educated psychopath be willing to kill for billions of dollars?

The potential for conspiracy does not prove conspiracy. But look at these facts:

In 1931, Dr. Otto Warburg won the Nobel Prize in physiology. He had been nominated 47 times for this award. Dr. Joseph Mercola writes, "Without a doubt the most powerful essential strategy I know of to treat cancer is to starve the cells by depriving them of their food source. Unlike your body cells, which can burn carbs or fat for fuel, cancer cells have lost that metabolic flexibility. Dr. Otto Warburg was actually given a Nobel Prize over 75 years ago for figuring this out but virtually no oncologist actually uses this information."

Why would oncologists not use this simple fact to help their patients? Quite possibly, many of them have never heard of the cancer cures available, or have been warned against them. Simply calling all of them "quackery" is enough to keep many otherwise good doctors from investigating further. Remember the knee-jerk reaction to the word "conspiracy?"

Other possible cancer cures were promoted by Dr. Max Gerson (1920s), Harry Hoxsey (1936–1963), Canadian nurse Rene Caisse (1920–1942), and two-time Nobel laureate Linus Pauling (1970s–1990s).

Linus Pauling was the only person ever to win two unshared Nobel Prizes (chemistry 1954 and peace 1962). He was also declared one of the top 20 scientists of all time (Simmons). His record and authority does not necessarily make him right on his own cancer treatment—using large doses of vitamin C, but it should say something for the credibility of his research. In 2004, Dr. Hilary Roberts wrote an article titled, "Vitamin C, Linus Pauling was right all along. A doctor's opinion." In her article, she reviews the work of Pauling's critics and analyzes the major flaws in their methodology.

If these so-called cancer cures had the success rates claimed by those who originated them, then most of the estimated 235 million people worldwide to die from cancer since 1925 would not have died from cancer.

Because of greed, these treatments were not given proper attention and analysis. Either by incompetence or greed, those who performed studies of Pauling's claims failed to prove their cases, yet the medical establishment continues to cite their flawed studies as proof against Pauling's cancer treatment.

Like the high priests of old, today's "science elite" may be sweeping real science under the rug in favor of more lucrative corporate or political dogma. The cost of this way of doing things proves to be far more expensive than war itself. Twentieth century wars killed roughly 142 million. Medical greed may have killed far more than twice as many people during the same century.

Unless you have a degree in the appropriate sciences, it becomes increasingly difficult to determine who is telling the truth. The old saying, "Follow the money," makes for an interesting substitute. Yet even this can be misleading, at times. A crafty, rich conspirator could salt the trail with conflicting evidence of enrichment. In order to unravel the knots of knowledge with so many conflicts of interest involved, we each need to improve our critical thinking skills.

Cancer statistics are also suspect. Why? Because the currently accepted mainstream methods for treating cancer involve radiation and chemotherapy, both of which remain potentially lethal in and of themselves. How many cancer patients actually died from the treatment, instead of the cancer? Yet, they are counted as cancer deaths, instead of treatment deaths.

Warburg's idea of starving the cancer cells can be implemented simply by adjusting the patient's diet. Thankfully, his research came long before the apparent corporate takeover of science.

How many conspiracies are involved in the health game? When conversations are held which bend rules, or even establish rules that jeopardize public health, those are very real conspiracies. And the deaths are very real, too.

Corrupt Congress

When legislative bills are rushed through the approval process without congressmen having the ability to read them, someone is not doing their job properly. Who makes those decisions? When they discuss making those decisions, they are conspiring. Not giving congressmen the time to read the bills upon which they vote is unethical in the extreme. The persons making the decision to vote too early may want the bills to pass. Could such bias be involved? If so, then voting is no longer democracy, but tyranny. Democracy is being strangled.

When those who write the bills include other topics or riders that have nothing to do with the main topic of a bill, that remains a questionable practice.

Increasingly, congress members no longer work for the people they are supposed to represent; they work for the corporations which give them the most funding. In Washington, DC, there are a couple dozen lobbyists for each member of Congress. Millions of dollars are spent giving American legislators perks. To expect that the legislators will not give something in return is naive at best. Only a few congresspersons have refused to see any lobbyists. Yet, a few legislators have hired lobbyists to work in their offices so that they remain closer to their funding sources.

In a very real sense, the chickens have invited the foxes into their hen house. Every conversation remains a potential conspiracy (Martin).

Health legislation is written by health industry lobbyists. Food legislation is written by food lobbyists. Drug legislation is written by drug lobbyists.

There is no disagreement that legislators need input from experts, but the method they're using is not above reproach.

Corrupt White House

It seems that promises by presidential candidates have become entirely meaningless. Sweet sounding rhetoric rings hollow, because the moment the new president steps into office, the promises are forgotten. Why do people still cheer? Are they that naive? Or have the crowds been rented? Are all those cheers from reasonably good actors?

There's far more going on here than merely breaking promises. When President Obama won the Nobel Peace Prize before he had done much of anything as president, the value of Nobel prizes seemed to evaporate. When Obama went on to become the most war-mongering president in American history, cognitive dissonance reached a fever pitch. Peace prize for a warmonger? Does this seem like manipulation of the masses? Remember Orwell's "doublethink?"

The American political parties have their differences, but those differences remain largely superficial. Both the Democrats and the Republicans are practically the same on all of the key national issues. They both want more,

- Wars of aggression
- Overspending and massive debt
- Tyranny and the continual erosion of liberties
- Protecting the big corporations
- Dismissal of the individual citizen

The 2012 presidential conventions of both major parties included unethical behavior on the part of the party leaders. Who exactly did this remains unclear, but both conventions demonstrated how corrupt the process has become. In both conventions, the speaker polling for a vote on issues before the convention body ignored the votes and followed a prearranged script. In the case of the Democratic convention, former Los Angeles Mayor, Antonio Villaraigosa, asked for a recount twice, because the votes from the audience did not match the script on his teleprompter (Swann). Whoever wrote that script and anyone involved in producing it all committed conspiracies to derail the voting process at the convention.

In the case of the Republican convention, one critical vote was going to be held on party procedures. The opposition was en route to the convention center when their bus driver kidnapped them, driving round and round the block until the vote was completed. Did the bus driver decide to do this on their own, or did someone discuss this with them ahead of time? A discussion on this matter would have been a conspiracy.

The People Speak—Surprise Congressional Response

A vast majority of the American public want their food properly labeled, especially for GMOs. According to an ABC news poll in 2014, 93% of Americans wanted GMOs labeled. What does Congress do? They pass the "Safe and Accurate Food Labeling Act of 2015." Sounds good, right? The only problem is, the bill that was passed *prevents* GMOs from being properly labeled. More cognitive dissonance. The name on the bill does not match the reality of its contents.

Several congressmen—the leaders on this issue—each made more than $100,000 in campaign contributions from the Big Agro businesses which don't want GMOs labeled. Conflict of interest? Money has corrupted the legislative process. Nothing new there, but Americans seem to have rose colored glasses when it comes to their own government.

American citizens let their wishes be known, but their legislators in Washington had their own ideas.

There is no doubt that the yearly conspiracies in government number in the thousands, at the very least. They may even range in the millions or billions.

Corrupt CIA

Operation Mockingbird was an operation started in the 1950s to influence the American media, amongst all of their other illegal operations.

When President Reagan asked CIA Director William Casey what he thought the goal of the agency should be, Casey replied, "We'll know our disinformation program is complete when everything the American public believes is false." He made this statement in early February 1981, in the Roosevelt Room of the White House. Remember Orwell's *1984?*

Chapter 9:
By the Numbers

The following is a summary of the numbers for this informal study of conspiracies. The counts refer to the rough estimate of conspiracies committed in the area described. Each of these counts includes many assumptions and cannot be used quantitatively with any usable degree of accuracy. These quantities are meant only to give a general magnitude of the conspiracies in each category. Thus, they must be considered merely for qualitative analysis, not quantitative.

- 56,000—Americans dying from occupational diseases or on job injuries
- 1,237,144—International deaths from occupational diseases or on job injuries
- 2,000,000—Children forced into slavery every year
- 2,514,241—Children conspiring to do something unethical or illegal
- 2,595,492—Scientific fraud or questionable actions worldwide
- 18,428,571—NSA conspiracies per year
- 432,713—American crime conspiracies (FBI arrest statistics)
- 9,559,431—International crime conspiracies

- 1,272,600—American college cheating conspiracies
- 1,342,000—American non-college scholastic cheating conspiracies
- 60,720,000—Non-American scholastic cheating conspiracies
- 505,806—American doctors conspiring to prescribe drugs off-label
- 505,806—International doctors conspiring to prescribe drugs off label
- 1,758,621—American malpractice conspiracies
- 38,851,193—International malpractice conspiracies
- 40,000,000—Abortions worldwide
- 3,240,000,000—Illegal drug purchases
- 12,000,000,000—Acts of prostitution

The estimated total number of conspiracies stands at nearly 15.42 billion per year. Dividing this number by the number of seconds in a year (31,557,600) gives us approximately 489 conspiracies per second.

As mentioned earlier, a great number of conspiracy categories were not included, so the actual number of new conspiracies per second could be even higher.

Chapter 10:
Accident or
Cause-and-Effect?

Bad things sometimes happen because of the combined attitudes of people. They seem to be a product of human nature. No conspiracy is involved. Perhaps this can be said of something like gasoline prices. Then again, who really knows what goes on in OPEC meetings and Big Oil boardrooms? After all, profit is their key guideline. If they conspire to control prices for maximum profit, this would only be natural, but it would still be a conspiracy.

As we have seen, there are plenty of examples of explicit, known conspiracies. We also have fairly accurate estimates of implied conspiracies, like the number of illicit drug sales, each of which includes a conspiracy, because each sale takes a seller and a buyer.

Let us say for a moment that we did not have this evidence. For those who would dismiss conspiracies out of hand, simply because they know of no evidence, proves to be a poorly supported attitude. At best, insisting that conspiracies cannot be true is an argument to ignorance type logical fallacy. A lack of evidence never disproves anything. By the same token, it doesn't prove an idea, either. We have to accept the notion that, because people are naturally selfish, conspiracies are very possible. When we don't have evidence one way or the other, we have to admit that we simply do not know. Yet, we should never ignore human nature any more than we would want to ignore gravity.

The Desire for a Unified World

In the introduction, we gave a couple of quotes attributed to David Rockefeller. One remains unattested; the other came from his *Memoirs*. They tell of an ideal future where there will be one world. But ideal for whom?

I have long loved the idea of a Federation (*à la Star Trek*)—all of humanity cooperating under one banner. The United Nations is sort of like that. So is the New World Order talked about by George H.W. Bush in his speech on September 11, 1990.

So, what's the big deal? A lack of freedom and privacy, for starters. If you want to do your own thing, a singular, totalitarian government might not let you. If you disobey, you die. Sound harsh? In a one world government, you have no escape if such freedom is ever needed. There are no other countries. The concept of "refugee" disappears. You would remain a criminal-at-large, until you died of starvation or were caught and killed for your disobedience.

How can any psychopathic leader ever guarantee that everything will be all right? Perhaps they can guarantee that for themselves. Those at the bottom of the food chain will not be so lucky.

History of human nature has shown that such power is too easily corrupted. It reduces to the least common denominator of selfish whim on the part of those in power. If the elite want to build a new space station and you're in the way?

Tough. Your home is destroyed. But they may also destroy you, too. It may prove too expensive to build you a new home—or too much of a bother.

The missing ingredient in Rockefeller Nirvana is altruism —unconditional love, generosity, wisdom and compassion. Psychopaths have none. They have a selfish idea in their minds that seems right and true to them. Anything or anyone that gets in the way is fair game. Non-psychopaths are pawns to be used in whatever manner they see fit.

Rockefeller Madness

Any psychopath knows the difference between right and wrong, but they don't care.

Rockefellers have funded Planned Parenthood and the notion of "family" planning. But it's not a family if Planned Parenthood uses their preferred service of abortion. We've already mentioned that the Rockefellers may have funded Women's Liberation in order to destroy the family unit, and to control children through the state.

The Rockefellers also love the idea of population control and eugenics—allowing the births of a superior breed and the elimination of inferior people. But who determines who is superior and who is inferior. How do they know that the child of poverty won't one day become a world leader? How do they know that the son or daughter of uneducated parents won't one day find a cure for all disease or even death itself?

When Margaret Sanger founded Planned Parenthood, she had a philosophy compatible with that of Rockefeller eugenics.

"Birth control," said Sanger, "is not contraception indiscriminately and thoughtlessly practiced. It means the release and cultivation of the better racial elements in our society, and the gradual suppression, elimination and eventual extirpation of defective stocks—those human weeds which threaten the blooming of the finest flowers of American civilization"—"Apostle of Birth Control Sees Cause Gaining Here," *The New York Times*, 1923-04-08, p. XII.

So, are you a "weed" to these psychopaths?

In the publication, *Birth Control Review*, 1918–32, Sanger made it clear what her stance was on the subject of eugenics. "Eugenics is ... the most adequate and thorough avenue to the solution of racial, political and social problems.... The campaign for birth control is not merely of eugenic value, but is practically identical with the final aims of eugenics"—"The Eugenic Value of Birth Control Propaganda," October 1921, page 5.

In *The Pivot of Civilization* (1922), Sanger also wrote, "Eugenics aims to arouse the enthusiasm or the interest of the people in the welfare of the world fifteen or twenty generations in the future. On its negative side it shows us that we are paying for and even submitting to the dictates of an ever increasing, unceasingly spawning class of human beings who never should have been born at all—that the wealth of individuals and of states is being diverted from the development and the progress of human expression and civilization"—Chapter 8, "Dangers of Cradle Competition."

In *Margaret Sanger: An Autobiography* (1938), she continues to clarify her position, writing, "Eugenics, which had started long before my time, had once been defined as including free love and prevention of conception... Recently it had cropped up again in the form of selective breeding....

"I accepted one branch of this philosophy, but eugenics without birth control seemed to me a house built upon sands. It could not stand against the furious winds of economic pressure which had buffeted into partial or total helplessness a tremendous proportion of the human race. The eugenists wanted to shift the birth control emphasis from less children for the poor to more children for the rich. We went back of that and sought first to stop the multiplication of the unfit. This appeared the most important and greatest step towards race betterment"—Chapter 30, "Now Is the Time for Converse," pp. 374–375.

Planned Parenthood made the news in 2015 for the notion of selling baby body parts from the abortions per-formed. Public outrage called for defunding the organization. The federal government, however, pushed back with threats against individual state action.

Abortions, like it or not, are murder by definition—"the killing of one person by another." Scientists and legislators can attempt to weasel out of this quagmire, but they will fail. What grows in the womb is alive simply by the definition of life. It remains human, because it came from humans. Premeditated killing of another human is murder. America had legalized a form of murder. Every discussion to make that happen was a conspiracy.

But some think it should be okay, because that "foreign growth" within their belly is an inconvenience. They should worry about the possibility that they may one day become an inconvenience to others. Already, the psychopathic elite have made remarks like, "a great culling is about to begin," getting rid of the "useless eaters"—those using up "our resources." In their simple minds, those psychopathic elite already own the world. To them, killing millions or even billions is perfectly okay. With the legalization of murder, they came one step closer to attaining their sinister goals.

As Aaron Russo informed us, Nick Rockefeller said of the masses of people, "Why do you care about them? Care about your own family."

On 9/11

When Nick Rockefeller talked with Aaron Russo in late 2000, he mentioned that a big event was about to happen which would give us Iraq and Afghanistan.

We can ignore the implications of this, but why would we? Rockefeller did not explicitly admit to prior knowledge of 9/11, but the implication seems clear. Nothing else would have given America Iraq and Afghanistan. Only the events of 9/11 did that. Yet, if the Rockefellers had advanced knowledge, they may well have been involved in carrying out that event. And the choice of words is most telling—"...give us Iraq and Afghanistan." Who is this "us?" From David Rockefeller's memoirs, we know that he does not consider himself to be an American in spirit. He is pleased with "...working against the best interests of the United States." So, to the Rockefeller family, it would seem that "us" means the family and not America.

Apparently the country (America) went to war and took possession of those lands. The news made it seem that America's "peacekeeping action" was only there to restore order. America would "return" those countries to their people. But is this what really happened? *De facto* ownership can be just as effective as *de jure*.

If a psychopathic elite could murder innocent people as pawns in an international game of chess, what else are they capable of doing?

A favorite player in the circles of power, Henry Kissinger, once said that military men are just "dumb, stupid animals to be used as pawns in foreign policy" (Bernstein). That he would say this, brings shame to his 1973 Nobel Peace Prize. Has the Nobel committee been corrupt for so long or were they merely ignorant of Kissinger's darker side?

Who Did 9/11?

It seems clear, now, that al-Qaeda could not have done 9/11.

Of course, the planes slamming into the three buildings on that day seem too incredible to believe. The mind was so assaulted by this, that any explanation would have been better than none. But when you dig deeper into the data uncovered by independent researchers, you find out that three buildings collapsed in New York. The third—World Trade Center 7 (WTC7)—fell at perfect free fall for the first eight floors. This means that the solid steel structure offered zero resistance to the collapse. Nowhere in this universe does solid steel ever offer zero resistance. The only way WTC7 could have achieved perfect free fall was with the aid of explosives or thermitic charges.

National Geographic aired an experiment to debunk the notion that thermite could cut through a steel beam. Were they properly motivated to find a method of cutting through steel, or did they have a preexisting bias? They used a hundred pounds of thermite on a steel beam far smaller than those used in the World Trade Center towers. Their experiment failed to damage the steel beam. To their television audience, this would seem effectively to debunk any crazy conspiracy theories about the use of thermite to bring down all three buildings.

One YouTube video posted by 8real shows both the National Geographic experiment and that of Jonathan Cole, a professional engineer. Cole performed several experiments in his back yard, eventually finding a method for cutting through a steel beam, both horizontally and vertically and using about one and a half pounds of thermite—close to 1% of the quantity used by National Geographic. The popular magazine showed that it was impossible, yet one independent researcher, with limited funding, showed that it was not only possible, but with a far smaller quantity of simple, homemade thermite.

The 9/11 concrete dust included an estimated several tons of iron microspheres. Proponents of the official conspiracy theory suggest that these iron spheres could have come from melted steel wool, melted flakes of iron rust from the steel beams or from fly ash in the concrete. The problem with this is that there were not tons of steel wool or iron rust in the fire zones of any of the three buildings. This topic is discussed in greater detail in my book, *Favorable Incompetence: Shining a Light on 9/11*.

Several pieces of evidence support the use of a high-tech version of thermite, called super nano-thermate. Microscopic chips of unreacted nano-thermate were found in the 9/11 concrete dust. Fires continued to burn deep within the rubble pile weeks after 9/11. Normal office fires will stop burning within a day or two, especially deep within a debris pile, because they will become oxygen starved. But thermite and nano-thermate contain their own sources of oxygen. Indeed, they can burn under water.

The fact that the CIA was a major tenant of WTC7 means that the required fitting of their building with explosives or thermitic cutters would likely not have gone unnoticed. To suspect that al-Qaeda could have worked for weeks in a building containing the second-largest CIA office in the world seems very unlikely. It seems more likely that some within the agency knew about the demolition materials and perhaps were even involved in their placement. For those agents who are not corrupt, those in charge may have given them a plausible cover story for the work being done on the building. We have no way of knowing for certain. CIA whistleblowers remain rare, but some exist.

Debunkers (supporters of the official conspiracy theory) have come up with all manner of alternate explanations for these details. None of them actually debunk anything. Alternate explanations are not proof, especially when they explain only some evidence, but fail to explain other, contradictory evidence. The so-called debunkers celebrate victory, but it remains a false victory.

Fallout from American Aggression

Because of the 9/11 set of conspiracies, thousands of American soldiers died. Of course, the psychopathic elite, like Kissinger, think of the soldiers as "dumb, stupid animals." As Nick Rockefeller implied, they care only about their own families and consider others to be unworthy of compassion. More than that, hundreds of thousands of civilians died in the Middle East at the hands of the Americans. Just following orders!

Were War Crimes involved? World Health Organization statistics on leukemia rates show that the world hot spot for this disease resides in Iraq. The second hottest bed of leukemia is found in Afghanistan. And both of these two nations lead all others by a large margin. The main thing they have in common that their Muslim neighbors don't have is the invading Americans. Also, an alarming number of babies have been born in Iraq with birth defects. We've seen how the CDC could commit crimes against black men in the mid-twentieth century. Are the Americans performing more experiments on unsuspecting Iraqis and Afghanis? How deep do their crimes go?

All of these crimes are no accident. They were planned. Conspiracies led to wars based on lies. But did the lies also come from conspiracies? All it takes is two or more people talking about doing something unethical or illegal.

Chapter 11:
What the Future Holds

As this book has shown, conspiracies remain dirt common. There are at least 489 new conspiracies every second, day-in and day-out, all year long. This conservative figure excludes many conspiracies for which we have little or no reliable statistics.

Our figure of 489 new conspiracies per second is helpful only for its qualitative value. It helps to put the word "conspiracy" into the proper perspective.

As long as people remain selfish or self-concerned, there will always be conspiracies. People will always continue to want things they do not have and will be willing to include others in their scheming, yet they will not want to get caught, for the most part.

What We Can Do About Conspiracies

What do we do? We can do the same thing that can be done with all forms of evil—shine a light on it. When everyone knows the source of evil, they will shun it. They will withdraw their support. The evil will shrivel and die on its own in many cases.

You cannot cure disease which poisons the body by flooding it with more poison, contrary to the madness of modern medicine. You cannot cure hatred with more hatred. And you cannot stop selfishness with more selfishness.

If you have darkness, turn on the light. If you have self-concern, use unconditional love.

Conspiracies thrive on darkness, lies and misperception. Strengthen your ability to perceive and to think critically. Don't blind yourself by clinging to old ideas; always question your own authority and knowledge. Be willing to throw out everything. It's always easy to take back what still works in the new light of unbiased reason.

By questioning what you know, you are practicing humility. Restraint and humility are the key ingredients found in any quest for discovery, and that includes science. You cannot learn anything new, if you think you already know the answers.

Above all, give your unconditional love to the conspirators. They remain misguided children of creation. They are being spoiled brats who think they deserve more than their human siblings.

Wish for them all that they desire. How they gain their hearts desire may not match their own plans. While they may plot to kill and steal, we may wish for them to receive their desires by some other method. When we do this, we stop resisting evil. When we do this, we help heal the source of all conspiracies—self-concern.

Other books to consider:

'Shining a Light' series

Favorable Incompetence: Shining a Light on 9/11 by Rod Martin, Jr. How the official conspiracy theory is full of holes, and how that tragedy is becoming increasingly relevant.

Thermophobia: Shining a Light on Global Warming by Rod Martin, Jr. How the scare is upside-down. How science has become corrupted by big money and fancy marketing, and what we can do to protect our future.

Books on Solutions

The Spark of Creativity: How to Unleash a Flood of Ideas That Matter, Right Now by Rod Martin, Jr. Overcoming writer's block and every other possible barrier to your own creativity.

Instant Happiness: How to assert positive control over your own emotions by Rod Martin, Jr. It's all about taking charge of your life.

Discount available on most ebook titles at http://TharsisHighlands.WordPress.com.

Appendix

- Notes
- References
- About Rod Martin, Jr.
- Other Books by Rod Martin, Jr.
- Connect with Rod Martin, Jr.

Notes

This "Notes" section was added in May 2018 to provide clarification to some of the book's topics and to point out some corrections.

Introduction: Conspiracies are Dirt Ordinary

Who is Nick Rockefeller, really? It seems he is not part of the infamous Rockefeller family, after all. He is not listed amongst the descendents of John D. Rockefeller. Did he misrepresent himself to Aaron Russo? Or did he let Mr. Russo jump to that conclusion on his own? Mr. Rockefeller may not have been part of the rich family—perhaps only a distant cousin—but the things he said seemed to paint a dark picture of his more worldly cousins. That picture seemed to be consistent with the eugenicist nature of John D.'s children, and the globalist desires mentioned by David Rockefeller in his Memoirs.

What was Nick Rockefeller's purpose in contacting Mr. Russo? Was he merely on some ego trip? Was everything he said merely made up—a fantasy of his own creation? Or was he told these things and sent to Russo to repeat them?

Aaron Russo had already made a name for himself with six Academy Award nominations and two Golden Globe nominations. In 1996, he took his political views to the silver screen with his documentary, *Mad as Hell*. And in 1998, he ran for governor of Nevada. Russo did not fear the concept of "conspiracy." This would've made him a target of conspirators who wanted to keep their anonymity and secrecy. This also earned for him a fair amount of ridicule from those who found the concept uncomfortable or from those who wanted to perpetuate that discomfort.

Was Nick Rockefeller a plant? If so, what would have been the purpose? If enough of the population have a knee-jerk reaction to conspiratorial ideas, then feeding true conspiracies to someone like Russo might generate an automatic rejection of such ideas. Thus, anyone who talks of the Rockefellers being involved in such things would automatically be dismissed, because "polite folk" already dismiss Russo.

The notion of rolling out some Orwellian "Newspeak" to control the population involves a great deal of marketing savvy. Operation Mockingbird was supposedly an illegal CIA operation to do just that within the United States. Google—the online search giant—has been caught internally promoting this idea of manipulating entire populations through their search engine results. Computing Forever's YouTube channel gives a critique on Google's leaked video trumpeting their proposed campaign to do just that—"Google's Leaked Video on Mass Behaviour Modification" (https://youtube.com/watch?v=UqByX959pxg). Superior marketing requires a superior understanding of human nature and how people react to things. If my own knee-jerk reaction to the word "conspiracy" was a product of this type of manipulation, then I suggest that the science of population manipulation has become relatively sophisticated.

It remains quite possible that Nick Rockefeller was told those things by the more visible Rockefeller family and then sent to Nevada to ensnare Russo—using the entertainment-mogul-turned-politician to help the more prominent Rocke-fellers deflect suspicion from themselves with this "bouncer effect." Tell the truth to a person you can discredit. This is speculation, but it's based on the stated desires of David Rockefeller and the past involvement of the Rockefeller family in things like Planned Parenthood to weed out the undesir-ables of the world.

Some websites online paint Russo as a charlatan. Whether or not he was one, would never have anything to do with the veracity of the Nick Rockefeller claims. But combining Nick's wannabe status with the "charlatan" claims against Aaron, it becomes harder for some people to take Nick's claims seriously. Could this have been the reason for Nick's involvement with Aaron?

Was this an example of psychopathic cleverness on the part of the Rockefellers, or was it merely the product of some nobody (Nick) with a famous last name trying to inveigle himself into the limelight? We simply don't know. And because we don't know, we need to use restraint from jumping to any hasty conclusions one way or the other. For now, it's merely information without a conclusion.

Chapter 1: Kids Will Be Kids

The section, "Gangs and Conspiracies," was taken from my first-place, award-winning short story, "Toady" (Dutton Books Award, Los Angeles, 1996). I have edited a portion of it to fit the needs of this section.

Chapter 7: Skeptical Until it Pays

In the last section of the chapter, "Science by Consensus, Settled Science, Climate Change and Climate-Gate," corrections and clarifications have been made to the discussion of climate science. In the last three years, since this book's initial publication, I have learned a great deal more about "climate change," refining my own understanding of these issues.

I have clarified the reason why the Holocene has two estimates of duration, and corrected the timetable discussion of interglacial cool-down.

The Holocene has been in a slight cooling trend throughout most of its 11,600-year existence. Based on a graph of temperature proxies from GISP2 Greenland ice cores, our world has experienced a significant warm period roughly once every thousand years. How can temperature proxies from one location represent the entire world? Of all the locations on Earth, Greenland is the closest thing we have to a planetary thermometer with a built-in record of past temperatures. Greenland is at the heart of northern hemisphere glaciation—the region which determines whether or not we are in a glacial or interglacial period. And Greenland is close to the region which benefits from the powerful Gulf Stream which brings tropical warmth to the polar region.

The Pacific Ocean has nothing like it. And the southern hemisphere doesn't either.

The northern hemisphere has a far larger percentage of land than does the southern, so is subject to greater swings in temperature than the southern. Also, the southern hemisphere does not have large land masses next to the polar glaciation for extending the range of land ice coverage. Thus, Greenland is best suited to represent in its ice the state of Earth's temperature health over the last few hundred millennia.

After the warmest part of the Holocene—called the Holocene Optimum—temperatures slumped for a couple of thousand years, but then rebounded about 1,500 BC up to the Minoan Warm Period. Since that brief warm peak, temperatures have been on a far steeper decline—3,000 years of cooling. When the Minoan Warm Period ended, the rapid cooling may have been what destroyed the Mycenaean civilization and ushered in the Greek Dark Ages. Ironically, temperatures had fallen down to our current level in the Modern Warm Period. Global cooling always results in less rain, and agriculture depends on rain. The Greek Dark Ages showed signs of widespread famine which may be directly related to the steep cooling at the end of the Minoan Warm Period.

The Roman Warm Period, about a thousand years later, was not quite as warm as the Minoan. The peak of the Medieval Warm Period was cooler, still. And we know that the Modern Warm Period is the coldest of the Holocene's 10 major warm periods (1,000-year cycle), because of things like the Vikings growing crops in Greenland for nearly 500 years, and similar effects around the world.

References

Definitions supplied by http://yourdictionary.com/

8real. (June 15, 2011). "National Geographic Thermite
Whitewash Debunked." Retrieved on August 30, 2015
from https://youtube.com/watch?v=jvuQjRmXoVw
911Myths.com. (ND). "Back off bin Ladin." Retrieved on
August 18, 2015 from
http://911myths.com/html/back_off_bin_ladin.html
Ananova. (November 7, 2001). "US agents told to back off bin
Ladens." Retrieved on August 19, 2015 from
http://propagandamatrix.com/us_agents_told_to_backo
ff.html
Baker, Russ. (April 27, 2015). "Out-of-Control FBI to Former
Head of 9/11 Investigation: Butt out!" Retrieved on
August 15, 2015 from
http://whowhatwhy.org/2015/04/27/out-of-control-fbi-
to-former-head-of-911-investigation-butt-out/
Bazerman, Max H., and Ann E. Tenbrunsel. (April 2011).
"Ethical Breakdowns." Retrieved on August 28, 2015
from https://hbr.org/2011/04/ethical-breakdowns

Bernstein, Bob, and Carl Woodward. (1977). The Final Days. Simon and Schuster, New York.

Blumenthal, Ralph. (October 28, 1993). "Tapes Depict Proposal to Thwart Bomb Used in Trade Center Blast." Retrieved on August 15, 2015 from http://nytimes.com/1993/10/28/nyregion/tapes-depict-proposal-to-thwart-bomb-used-in-trade-center-blast.html

Broecker, Wallace. (1998). " The end of the present interglacial: How and when?" Quaternary Science Reviews, v. 17, p. 689–694.

Cartalucci, Tony. (February 17, 2012). "Washington DC: FBI Foils Own Terror Plot (Again)." Retrieved on August 15, 2015 from http://infowars.com/washington-dc-fbi-foils-own-terror-plot-again/

Cartalucci, Tony. (April 20, 2013). "FBI Casting Set Stage for Boston Marathon Bombing, Shootout, Charade." Retrieved on August 15, 2015 from http://infowars.com/fbi-casting-set-stage-for-boston-marathon-bombing-shootout-charade/

Census. (July 2007). Summary File 3. Retrieved on August 31, 2015 from http://census.gov/prod/cen2000/doc/sf3.pdf

Chandler, David. (January 29, 2014). "WTC7: NIST Finally Admits Freefall (Part I)." Retrieved on December 15, 2014 from https://youtube.com/watch?v=Rkp-4sm5Ypc

Civil Justice Resource Group. (ND). "Medical Malpractice... By the Numbers." Retrieved on August 10, 2015 from http://centerjd.org/cjrg/Numbers.pdf

Cook, John, et al. (May 15, 2013). "Quantifying the consensus on anthropogenic global warming in the scientific literature." Retrieved on September 1, 2015 from http://iopscience.iop.org/1748-9326/8/2/024024/article

Cook, Joshua. (April 16, 2015). "Sen. Bob Graham Says FBI went beyond 9/11 Cover-Up to 'Aggressive Deception'." Retrieved on August 15, 2015 from http://truthinmedia.com/sen-bob-graham-says-fbi-went-beyond-911-cover-up-to-aggressive-deception/

Dachel, Anne. (May 21, 2015). "Moms In Charge Presents Dr. Andrew Wakefield on CDC Whistleblower." Retrieved on September 1, 2015 from http://ageofautism.com/2015/05/moms-in-charge-presents-dr-andrew-wakefield-on-cdc-whistleblower.html

Eggen, Dan, and Miller, Bill. (May 24, 2002). "FBI Flaws Alleged by Field Staff." Retrieved on August 19, 2015 from http://propagandamatrix.com/fbi_flaws_alleged_by_field_staff.htm

Fanelli, Daniele. (May 29, 2009). "How Many Scientists Fabricate and Falsify Research? A Systematic Review and Meta-Analysis of Survey Data." Retrieved on July 30, 2015 from http://journals.plos.org/plosone/article?id=10.1371/journal.pone.0005738

Ferguson, Charles. (2010). Inside Job (documentary). Sony Pictures Classics, New York.

Heath, David. (June 3, 2013). "Erin Brockovich's Biggest Debunker, Debunked." Retrieved on August 28, 2015 from http://motherjones.com/environment/2013/05/erin-brockovich-hinkley-california-junk-science

Institute of Education Sciences (IES). (2015). "Back to School Statistics." Retrieved on August 12, 2015 from http://nces.ed.gov/fastfacts/display.asp?id=372

Jones, Alex. (August 24, 2009). "Aaron Russo: Reflections and
    Warnings." Retrieved on August 19, 2015 from
    https://youtube.com/watch?v=V2_lrZSbKwI

Joseph PhD., R. (May 29, 2002). "America Betrayed - Bush
    Administration, FBI Complicity In 911." Retrieved on
    August 18, 2015 from
    http://rense.com/general25/fb.htm

Langer, Gary. (June 19, 2014). "Poll: Skepticism of Genetically
    Modified Foods." Retrieved on August 12, 2015 from
    http://abcnews.go.com/Technology/story?id=97567

Lectric Law Library. (ND). "Combined report by Paul
    DeRienzo, Frank Morales and Chris Flash From
    newspaper _The_Shadow_ Oct. 1994/Jan. 1995 Issue."
    Retrieved on August 15, 2015 from
    http://lectlaw.com/files/cur46.htm

Liberty Beacon, The. (June 21, 2013). "New Published Study
    Verifies Andrew Wakefield's Research on Autism –
    Again (MMR Vaccine Causes Autism)." Retrieved
    September 1, 2015 from
    http://thelibertybeacon.com/2013/06/21/new-published-
    study-verifies-andrew-wakefields-research-on-autism-
    again-mmr-vaccine-causes-autism/

Martin, Jr., Rod. (April 8, 2015). "Lobbying in the United
    States — Foxes in the Hen House." Retrieved on April 8,
    2015 from http://uisio.com/lobbying-in-the-united-
    states-foxes-in-the-hen-house/

Maslen, Geoff. (February 19, 2012). "Worldwide student
    numbers forecast to double by 2025." Retrieved on
    August 12, 2015 from
    http://universityworldnews.com/article.php?story=2012
    0216105739999

Mercola, Dr. Joseph. (August 3, 2013). "Why Medicine Won't
    Allow Cancer to Be Cured." Retrieved on September 2,

2015 from
http://articles.mercola.com/sites/articles/archive/2013/08
/03/natural-cancer-treatment.aspx

NASA. (ND). "Scientific consensus: Earth's climate is
warming." Retrieved on July 27, 2015 from
http://climate.nasa.gov/scientific-consensus/

NumberOf.net. (ND). "Number of Malpractice Lawsuits in the
US per Year." Retrieved on August 10, 2015 from
http://numberof.net/number%C2%A0of%C2%A0malpr
actice%C2%A0lawsuits%C2%A0in-the-us-
per%C2%A0year/

Paul, Rand. (June 29, 2012). "Sen. Rand Paul Speaks Out
Against Senators Voting without Reading the Bills."
https://youtube.com/watch?v=svGDZOW-brA

Rappoport, Jon. (July 29, 2014). "FBI terrorists among us: the
1993 WTC Bombing." Retrieved on August 15, 2015
from
https://jonrappoport.wordpress.com/2014/07/29/fbi-
terrorists-among-us-the-1993-wtc-bombing/

Roberts, Dr. Hilary. (August 17, 2004). "Vitamin C, Linus
Pauling was right all along. A doctor's opinion."
Retrieved on September 2, 2015 from
http://medicalnewstoday.com/releases/12154.php

Rockefeller, David. (2002). Memoirs. Random House, New
York.

Simmons, John G. (2000). The Scientific 100: A Ranking of the
Most Influential Scientists, Past and Present. Citadel
Press, New York.

Sperry, Paul. (April 12, 2015). "How the FBI is whitewashing
the Saudi connection to 9/11." Retrieved on August 15,
2015 from http://nypost.com/2015/04/12/saudi-role-in-
911-being-whitewashed-by-fbi/

Stein, Jeff. (June 20, 2015). "FBI Agent: The CIA Could Have
    Stopped 9/11." Retrieved on August 18, 2015 from
    http://informationclearinghouse.info/article42198.htm
Storm Clouds Gathering. (January 23, 2013). "Fake Skeptics &
    The 'Conspiracy Theorist' Slur." Retrieved August 15,
    2014 from https://youtube.com/watch?v=0BJA1R8YIHk
Stratford, Michael. (ND). "Why Were the 9/11 Pentagon Tapes
    Seized by the FBI?" Retrieved on August 15, 2015 from
    http://classroom.synonym.com/were-9-11-pentagon-
    tapes-seized-fbi-18501.html
Swann, Ben. August 23, 2012. "Reality Check: RNC Pulling
    Out All Stops To Keep Ron Paul's Name Out Of
    Nomination." Retrieved on March 22, 2015 from
    https://youtube.com/watch?v=cQvszfnOSY8
Swann, Ben. August 30, 2012. "Did RNC 'Scripted' Rules
    Change Start A Civil War In The Republican Party?"
    Retrieved on March 22, 2015 from
    https://youtube.com/watch?v=pKaXqoC4DjE
Swann, Ben. September 6, 2012. "Reality Check: DNC Runs
    Over Delegates With Scripted Platform Vote."
    Retrieved on March 22, 2015 from
    https://youtube.com/watch?v=HmaE2Aez_XY
Talboo, John-Michael. (November 29, 2008). "Debunking 9/11
    Conspiracy Debunkers with Stewart Bradley."
    Retrieved on August 18, 2015 from
    http://911truth.org/debunking-911-conspiracy-
    debunkers-with-stewart-bradley/
WarCrime911. (October 15, 2011). "9/11 Suspects - Explosive
    Connections (Updated Fixed and Revised)." Retrieved
    on August 19, 2015 from
    https://youtube.com/watch?v=ffs7PkOREEY [3:32]
Watts, Anthony. (September 3, 2013). "Cooks '97% consensus'
    disproven by a new peer reviewed paper showing

major math errors." Retrieved on September 1, 2015 from http://wattsupwiththat.com/2013/09/03/cooks-97-consensus-disproven-by-a-new-paper-showing-major-math-errors/

Watts, Anthony. (June 11, 2015). "Climate Fraud - NOAA's Global Temperature Dataset." Lecture viewed on July 26, 2015 from https://youtube.com/watch?v=pjlPvwRP-fM

Weiss, Murray. (2003). The Man Who Warned America. HarperCollins Publishers, New York.

World Health Organization. (February 2015). "Cancer." Retrieved on September 2, 2015 from http://who.int/mediacentre/factsheets/fs297/en/

World Population Clock. (ND). "Current World Population." Retrieved on August 25, 2015 from http://worldometers.info/world-population/

Wright, Lawrence. (January 14, 2002). "The Counter-Terrorist." Retrieved on September 14, 2015 from http://newyorker.com/ magazine/ 2002/01/14/the-counter-terrorist

About Rod Martin, Jr.

Rod Martin, Jr. is a teacher, software engineer with a degree *summa cum laude,* a Hollywood artist with screen credit, and a published author of both fiction and non-fiction. He was born into a religious family in West Texas. His mother was the daughter of a Southern Baptist minister. His father was a student of Eastern mysticism and philosophy, frequently reading of reincarnation and karma, but also from the Bible. His father had also been a high school science teacher and manager of a NASA contract division at Doc. Inc., College Park, Maryland.

Mr. Martin went on to study art, electronic engineering, computer software, Buddhism, Judaism, the Kabbalah and back to Christianity.

With a life full of experiences, he has had many opportunities to increase his understanding of reality and truth.

His first career involved graphic arts including professional typography, fine art and matte paintings for a Hollywood film. He enjoyed several one-person shows of his space-related art.

With the proliferation of personal computers, Mr. Martin switched careers to that of computer systems and software engineering. He gained a bachelors degree summa cum laude in computer information technology, and worked for Control Data Corporation, Ceridian Payroll, Bank of America, Global Database Marketing and IPRO Tech.

From a lifelong love of stars and astronomy, he created 3D space software, "Stars in the NeighborHood," available online.

He currently resides in the Philippines with his wife, Juvy.

He has taught mathematics, information technology, critical thinking and professional ethics at Benedicto College, Mandaue City, Cebu. He continues to teach online and to write.

Other Books by Rod Martin, Jr.

Non-Fiction (as Rod Martin, Jr.)

The Art of Forgiveness, Tharsis Highlands (2012, 2015)

The Bible's Hidden Wisdom: God's Reason for Noah's Flood, Tharsis Highlands (2014)

The Spark of Creativity, Tharsis Highlands (2014)

Dirt Ordinary: Shining a Light on Conspiracies, Tharsis Highlands (2015)

Favorable Incompetence: Shining a Light on 9/11, Tharsis Highlands (2015)

Thermophobia: Shining a Light on Global Warming, Tharsis Highlands (2016)

Red Line—Carbon Dioxide: How humans saved all life on Earth by burning fossil fuels, Tharsis Highlands (2016)

The Science of Miracles: How Scientific Method Can Be Applied to Spiritual Phenomena, Tharsis Highlands (2018)

Proof of God, Tharsis Highlands (2018)

Deserts & Droughts: How does Land Ever Get Water?, Tharsis Highlands (2018)

Taking Charge: How to Assert Positive Control Over Your Own Emotions, Tharsis Highlands (2018)

Spirit is Digital—Science is Analog: Discovering where miracles and logic intersect, Tharsis Highlands (2019)

Proof of Atlantis? Evidence of Plato's Lost Island Empire, Tharsis Highlands (2019)

Enemies of Christ: The Need to Protect Our Own Salvation from Ravening Wolves, Tharsis Highlands (2019)

Science Fiction (as Carl Martin)

Touch the Stars: Emergence, with John Dalmas, Tor (1983), *expanded* Tharsis Highlands (2012)

Touch the Stars: Diaspora, Book 2 of Touch the Stars, Tharsis Highlands (2014)

Entropy's Children, anthology of short fiction, Tharsis Highlands (2014)

Gods and Dragons, Book 1 of *Edge of Remembrance*, Tharsis Highlands (2017)

Tales of Atlantis Lost, Book 2 of *Edge of Remembrance*, Tharsis Highlands (2017)

Excerpt from
Favorable Incompetence: Shining a Light on 9/11

Introduction: The Official Conspiracy Theory

Why bother with 9/11? Isn't it "old news?"

Think for a moment. First of all, any book of history can prove valuable. If it shines a new light on events and helps us to see things from a new viewpoint, that can help prepare us for the future.

But 9/11 is a current event. Like a raging forest fire that has not yet been extinguished, 9/11 keeps delivering new tragedies. With every law written that makes one more tear in the Constitution—with every new battle or skirmish in the never-ending and lucrative War on Terror—and with every other government action which uses 9/11 as a reason—that day of ruin continues to wreck havoc on our world. September 11 is still very much alive and active.

A Theory Full of Holes

Isn't it ironic. The American government makes such a big deal out of dismissing conspiracy theories, but had no problem dispensing their own theory for the world to believe. When a citizen lies to the government, they go to prison; when the government lies, it's merely politics as usual.

If you think conspiracies never happen, think again. In my book, Dirt Ordinary: Shining a Light on Conspiracies, I detail hundreds of facts which show how such things are as common as ordinary dirt.

The official conspiracy theory goes something like this:

Nineteen men, armed with box cutters, hijacked four airliners, overpowering the passengers and military trained pilots.

With minimal pilot training and insufficient skills to rent a propeller airplane, they flew their highly complex, jumbo jet aircraft at more than a hundred miles per hour above the maximum operating velocity for sea level flight and expertly crashed their airplanes into their targets. Yet, even the experts say that such accuracy is near impossible for a seasoned pilot and that the structural integrity of their airplanes would likely have failed before they could have reached their targets.

All of this was orchestrated by a single madman, operating a laptop and a cell phone in a cave fortress in Afghanistan half a world away, breaking through the Trillion dollar defenses of the world's mightiest military without being molested by a single fighter interceptor.

The two crashes in New York, resulted in the complete, catastrophic and vertical collapse of three steel framed buildings, killing nearly 3,000 people.

In Virginia, one plane broke through the most highly protected airspace on the planet to circle the Pentagon in a 270°, descending corkscrew turn to come level with the ground in order to crash into the recently upgraded and least populated wedge of the building, far from the offices of the top brass. In the area of destruction, many accountants were busy working on the puzzle of the missing $2.3 Trillion that Defense Secretary Donald Rumsfeld had announced on the day before, September 10, 2001.

The Great Danger

The greatest danger with 9/11 was that it triggered an emotional reaction that destroyed the liberty of all American citizens. Another danger revealed by 9/11 is that the government can kill its own citizens in order to achieve a desired objective—a reason to go to war—a perpetual war that will make some corporations extremely wealthy while killing thousands in the American military, and millions in the countries suffering American unilateral aggression.

A favorite player in the circles of power, Henry Kissinger, once said that military men are just "dumb, stupid animals to be used as pawns in foreign policy" (Bernstein). Kissinger had been Bush's first choice to lead the 9/11 Commission. How many in government have his attitude about military men? Too many, it seems.

The danger remains that the government could give us another 9/11 at any time. Don't believe this?

If you don't believe that the American government can betray its own people, then look back through history....

https://tharsishighlands.wordpress.com/books/favorable-incompetence-911/

Connect with Rod Martin, Jr.

Rod Martin, Jr. is his pen name for non-fiction. Carl Martin is his pen name for fiction.
BitChute—https://bitchute.com/channel/M63WrjRpNSPT/
Minds—https://minds.com/RodMartinJr
Gab—https://gab.ai/RodMartinJr
Website and Blog—https://rodmartinjr.wordpress.com/
HubPages—https://hubpages.com/@lone77star
Smashwords author page—
https://smashwords.com/profile/view/CarlMartin77
Smashwords author page—
https://smashwords.com/profile/view/RodMartinJr
Udemy courses page—https://udemy.com/user/rodmartinjr/
Facebook—https://facebook.com/RodMartinJr/
Twitter—https://twitter.com/LoneStar77/
YouTube—https://youtube.com/c/RodMartinJr/
Goodreads author page—https://goodreads.com/Carl_Martin
Goodreads author page—
https://goodreads.com/Rod_Martin_Jr
Amazon author page—https://amazon.com/Carl-
Martin/e/B008CX8KN6/

Amazon author page—https://amazon.com/Rod-Martin-
   Jr/e/B008CZ9JTS/

Websites

Science
https://AncientSunsBlog.WordPress.com/
https://GlobalWarmthBlog.WordPress.com/
https://MissionAtlantis.WordPress.com/
https://RodMartinCriticalThinking.WordPress.com/
https://SpaceSoftware.WordPress.com/

Politics
https://AndThePursuitOfHappinessBlog.WordPress.com/

Education
https://InfinityDynamics.WordPress.com/
https://TharsisHighlands.WordPress.com/

Spirit
https://GenesisCodeBlog.WordPress.com/
https://RodMartinLoveOfGod.WordPress.com/